THE
PARADOX

A guide to being unstoppable

For Those Who Dare To Be Different

ANAWO MATHIAS

*Whatever adversity we face in life, it is for good
And it is our duty to make it good.*

CONTENTS

CHAPTER FOUR
ENGAGE IN CONFLICT

FOREWORD

When Marcus Aurelius wrote the *meditations*, it was not because he wanted to be a published author but instead, it was a means of expressing his suffering and admonishing himself to do what was right and not cave into panic and fear. Seneca while on exile also found solace in writing the *consolations*. Paul the apostle who was a pharisee turn radical preacher of the gospel faced many challenges in his new resolution which included trials and prison sentences, being beaten and dragged out of the city, being on the run for almost his entire ministerial life due to amount of people sorting to kill him even in all these tribulations Paul found solace in writing, he wrote fourteen out of the twenty-seven books of the new testament, it was a way of exorcising his frustration, keeping himself sane and admonishing the church to not waver in faith. The paradox is one such book whose primary aim is for the edification of the writer, to admonish him and keep him sane so that he does not waver in faith and begin to panic.

Growing up as a child I was a different kid amongst my siblings, I have three siblings who are mild and agreeable while I was the direct opposite, adventurous and unagreeable because of this I received a lot of sticks and got into a lot of fights meant to make me conform.

My dad was my hero and solace, he inflamed me with belief and taught me how to dream, with him the future was always picture perfect, unfortunately, he passed away before my age could reach a double digit.   I was never a fan of the conventional life; I always wanted more adventure and freedom so I dreamt big as my dad taught me and with big dreams comes great suffering and with great suffering comes great enlightenment. Maneuvering a world where I didn't feel like I fit in and chasing a dream that the odds were not in my favour, I was at risk of living a pathetic life. It is in this struggle that I realized that the uncertainty and suchness of our world were for good and it is our duty to make it good. I also realized that a unidimensional approach to life is not only limiting but sometimes an opposition to life itself.

This book contains counterintuitive wisdom that will help you in building resilience and maintaining calmness and clarity in the face of adversity. It teaches taking responsibility for the course of one's life and having a fluid multidimensional approach to life so that as long as you live you are always optimal no matter the circumstance. The lessons within this book are crafted from personal experience, ancient philosophical wisdom, scientific research, and religious studies. The lessons within this book includes

- How to maintain stillness and clarity in the face of adversity and uncertainty
- How to overcome anxiety and fear and succeed under pressure
- How to heal from your childhood trauma and overcome your limiting believes
- How to use deliberate practice to stand out in your career and increase your chances for success.
- How to deal better with conflict
- How to live effortlessly and avoid stress
- How to avoid being a victim of life.
-

The pages that follow tells the stories of men and women who were just like you, who struggled as you struggled amid the overwhelming pressures of life but still managed to succeed with so much poise and integrity. You will be learned about the trials and triumphs of Jesus Christ, James Stockdale, Nelson Mandela, Mohammed Ali, Christiano Ronaldo, Tiger woods, Linda ikeji, Usman dan Fodio.

We will study keenly the life of these great men and learn from the strategies they use to achieve greatness. We would also delve into the ancient Asian philosophy of Taoism and learn from the wisdom of the great Zen master Lao Tzu and the works of other authors.

CHAPTER ONE

BE INDIFFERENT

"This is a very important lesson you must never confuse faith that you would prevail at the end which you can never afford to lose with discipline to confront the most brutal facts of your current reality whatever that might be"
James Stockdale.

A happy man is too satisfied with the present to dwell on the future
Albert Einstein

THE STOCKDALE PARADOX

James bond Stockdale was born on the 23rd of December 1923 in Abingdon, Illinois, USA. He attended the US naval academy where he attained a B.sc degree and graduated on the 5th of June 1946, he was then assigned, as an assistant gunnery officer.

After twenty years in the navy, Stockdale decided to enroll in a two-year graduate program at Stanford University where he began the study of philosophy under World War II commander Philip Rhinelander.

After the final class knowing that Stockdale was graduating and returning to the cockpit and also grossly impressed by his interest in philosophy and ancient wisdom. Rhinelander gave Stockdale a gift that change the course of his life it was a copy of the stoic philosopher Epictetus's book known as the *Enchiridion.*

Over the next three years, Stockdale pondered on the teachings of stoicism and always kept the Enchiridion within arms-length. During this period the US military was at the forefront of the Vietnamese war. Stockdale boarded aircraft carriers across the western pacific and launched cruises to the waters of Vietnam. He led the first-ever
 American bombing raid against North Vietnam. He commanded the USS Oriskany also nicknamed the mighty O.
While on a raid in north Vietnam on the 9th of September 1965 his war aircraft the A-4 Skyhawk was shot down by Vietnamese forces. In his thirty seconds midair ejection from the Skyhawk Stockdale whispered to himself "five years down there at least I am leaving the world of technology and I am entering into the world of Epictetus"
He landed in a village in north Vietnam and was greeted by Vietnamese forces who tortured him mercilessly and took him as a prisoner of war.

Stockdale was arrested with several of his colleagues and were all held prisoners at the infamous Hanoi Hilton prison in north Vietnam. Over the last three years, the word of Epictetus had taught him the importance of the autonomy and freedom of his mind, that it is something that cannot be taken away from him no matter the circumstances of life. In the golden words of Epictetus, "a podium and a prison are each a place one high and the other low but in either place, your freedom of choice can be maintained if you so wish"

 with this word on a kind of internal loop Stockdale found resilience and his captivity became an adventure, fate has finally allowed him to practice his philosophy, in a later interview he said

"I never got depressed because I never wavered in my faith that not only will I get out but I will turn that moment into a defining period of my life, that in retrospect I won't trade"

Being the most senior military officer among the prisoners of war, he was subjected to the harshest of torture, he was kept in solitary confinement and his broken leg were bounded with leg irons but this did not deter Stockdale's pragmatism and clarity, while in prison he refused to release vital information about the American military to Vietnamese forces on one occasion he slit his wrist open to avoid being tortured, he created and enforced a code of conduct for all the prisoners that governed torture, he created a secret code of communications for all prisoners. When told by his captors that he was to be paraded in public, he slit his scalp with a razor to purposely disfigure himself so that his captors do not use him for propaganda. when they covered his head with a hat, he beat himself with a stool until his face was swollen beyond recognition.

Stockdale learned to live without fear or hope as the stoics teach believing that fear and hope are the flipsides of the same coin, a pointless concern for future events. Most of his fellow prisoners of war as he noticed tormented themselves with hope.

When the author Jim Collins who is known for popularizing the concept of the *Stockdale paradox* in his book *Good to Great* asked Stockdale which of his fellow prisoner of war did not make it out of Hanoi Hilton Stockdale replied "oh that is easy, the optimist"

This reply confused Jim Collins as it seems to counter what Stockdale said earlier when he talked about having unwavering faith in getting released which sounded optimistic "you sounded optimistic" Jim said referring to their earlier conversation "no I was not optimistic, I never wavered in my faith that in the end I will prevail but I was not optimistic" replied Stockdale, then what is the difference? Asked Jim Collins. Stockdale replied "the optimist were the ones who said we are going to be out by

Christmas and Christmas would come and Christmas would go, then they would say we are going out by Easter and Easter would come and Easter would go and then thanksgiving and then it would be Christmas again and they died of a broken heart"

Stockdale then grab Jim's shoulder and said sternly "this is what I learned when you are faced with great calamity and uncertainty you have to on one hand never confuse the need for unwavering faith that you will find a way to prevail in the end with on the other hand the discipline to confront the most brutal facts you face"

Stockdale's indifference and pragmatism helped him to confront the grim reality of his situation without giving in to despair or depression, he realized only the ruthless acceptance of the present would sustain him over the long haul. He knew that as long as he focused on what was within his control and play well the role fate has given him and not given into hope of an early release something which was outside his control, he would prevail no matter the outcome. So, casting away all thoughts of future fears or hope, he believed instead that the only harm that could be done to him would be done by himself.

With this powerful blend of radical realism and faith, he made it out of Hanoi Hilton. he was released during operation homecoming on the

12th of February 1973 after spending seven years in captivity and was barely able to walk due to the dilapidating treatment he received in captivity. He received so many accolades for his heroics in north Vietnam which included twenty-seven combat awards and a promotion to vice admiral of the US navy.

When our suffering has an impending end, it is much easier to cope with but when the prospects of an end are no longer feasible or left to uncertainty we cope badly, we become unstable, and suffer in our imaginations. hope makes us feel alive, it gives resilience in the face of a challenge and the motivation to do work but these emotions radiated by feeling hopeful are fragile because they thrive on prospects, likelihoods, and anticipation of things beyond our control. The moment these likelihoods vanishes it results in a rude awakening that causes a great depression, demotivation, and a sense of purposelessness. So, this makes us human beings as hopeful as we are fearful, and vice versa. The more you hope for a certain outcome which is driven by the likelihood of it happening the more you fear losing those likelihoods or the outcome. In simple terms the more you hope for an outcome the more you dread an opposite or even an alternative outcome.

This is because even as optimistic as being hopeful is, it thrives on the probability of things not happening, for example, a couple who is expecting the birth of their child and has gone for an ultrasound scan will not be hopeful about the gender of that child they already know the gender no need to torment their mind with a preference for a particular gender, in other words there is no hope because there is no probability of negation. An optimist is just a counterintuitive pessimist and vice versa, both are not the best approach for long-term resilience.

If calamity is to really test you, neither optimism nor pessimism stands a chance in granting you fortitude, they are both short-term games. For some of Stockdale's optimistic colleagues, the hope for an early release kept them resilient for maybe the first three years but immediately the likelihood of a release was no longer feasible and freedom was left to uncertainty they fell into depression and died. Even if they did the opposite which is being pessimistic, they would have been met with the same or an even more fatal fate. What made Stockdale a survivor was not pessimism or optimism but sheer pragmatism and indifference, the acceptance of *what is* and doing well the things within his control. This is the basis of *stoic philosophy*.

The ruling reason behind stoic philosophy is the *dichotomy of control* which teaches that as long as a person focuses on what is in their control and does not concern themselves with what is outside their control, they will maintain their freedom of choice no matter the circumstance. What are the things within your control? your perceptions and actions(effort) what are the things outside of your control? Other people's perceptions and actions, outcomes (results), and fate. In plain terms as long as you do well the things within your powers you will always prevail in the end no matter the outcome even if it is the bleakest of outcomes. This is what Stockdale meant when he said he had unwavering faith that he will prevail at the end.

You might never in your life become a prisoner of war such as Stockdale or be a slave such as Epictetus or go through harsh imperial sufferings as in ancient Rome that forged the stoics, due to the stability and technological advancement of our present world which has made our life much easier compared to those who lived before us but this doesn't mean we are without our problems and individual challenges. As the author Jim Collins pointed out we are always in a Stockdale moment and this means we also need great fortitude and resilience in other to live a meaningful, productive, and fulfilled life. This means you need to develop a backbone of indifference which means having the bravery to see the effect of circumstances and their outcomes as secondary, something subject to your choice of virtue (action and perception) with these comes great clarity and a sense of adventure even in the face of brutal adversity or uncertainty. knowing where to focus your energy and having the discipline not to concern yourself with what is outside your control. This leads to progression in overcoming challenges and achieving ambitions.

To be truly resilient and indifferent to the suchness of the realities of life one must rid the mind of hope and fear and replace them with curiosity in the effect of practicing what is in one's control. It creates discipline and perseverance and clarity; it can make an adventure out of adversity and break down long-term goals into basic simple steps that one can follow. The major difference between curiosity and hope is that curiosity doesn't need the presence of likelihood of an outcome as a motivation. Curiosity is so effective in productivity and resilience because it concerns itself with the effect of accumulated effort over time without giving in to hope for a particular outcome but instead grounding a person in present-moment awareness. When Stockdale was forced to eject his war aircraft, he perfectly understood what adversity he was going to face but instead of giving into despair or hope for a better treatment, he was curious about practicing his philosophy and about what lessons he was going to learn, he saw an opportunity to practice the freedom of his choice and become a better stoic. By being curious about his actions he didn't care how long his suffering endured or if he was even going to survive, his curiosity in his own choice transmuted a calamity into an adventure.

The author and renowned marine soldier David Golgins said "when life put me in a dark place, I don't panic I study it" only those who are curious and who don't give-in to panic or hope for a better fate can have the fortitude to study the darkness and become better as a result of it. It is in overcoming hurdles that we become better and our skill set either physical or mental becomes refined.

It's also with curiosity that we can achieve the toughest of ambitions. Obsession can give us the drive to achieve an objective but since it thrives on hope and hope is motivated by the presence of a likelihood, it is emotional and fleeting and not ideal for long-term rigorous work. Any objective or ambition that yields a good number of dividends is usually tough and requires a long-term rigorous work ethic and dedication. For a person to achieve a great ambition he needs discipline and not necessarily obsession. Discipline is built from curiosity in the accumulation of present-moment effort and not the outright outcome of effort.

When we focus on results rather than our efforts it results in willful will and agitation, the mind is then not stable to do anything creative, we get in our own way. Focusing on outcomes paralysis the action we take in the present moment. When Olympic athletes compete for a gold medal, they can't stop to think how pretty the medal is, they have to flow with the present moment, if they lose focus for a second thinking how proud they will be to show the medal to their parent, they will certainly commit an error at critical moments and will not win the competition.

The Taoist philosopher Lao Tzu gave a story of an archer who made a fool of himself by focusing too much on the price. "he who is contending for a piece of earthenware put forth all his skills, if the price be for a buckle of brass he shoots timorously if it is for an article of gold, he shoots as if he were blind. The skill of the archer is the same in all cases but in the two later cases he is under the influence of solitude and looks on external price as most important, all who attach importance to what is external show stupidity in themselves"

The great Zen master and archery teacher Awa Kenzo always made sure he taught his student the importance of letting go of the mental attachment of hitting the targets and the importance of getting lost in the entire process of archery.

He spent almost no time instructing his student on how to deliberately aim and shoot, telling them to simply draw a shot back until it "fell from you like a ripe fruit" what Kenzo wanted his student to do was to put away the obsession of hitting the target out of their minds. He wanted them to detach from the idea of an outcome. The hit on the target he would say was just an outward proof and confirmation of purposelessness in its purest form. Kenzo was trying to inculcate in his students the importance of mastering the basics which are often boring but fundamental to being a good archer and hitting the target was just a natural outcome of honouring the entire learning process.

In the blockbuster movie karate kid, when Jaden smith who acted as the karate kid started learning kung Fu, he was frustrated by the fact that all his master told him was to routinely take off his jacket and put it back on while he sat at distance and almost paying no attention, after doing only that for a couple session he was no longer having it and he angrily lashed out "I put my jacket on a thousand times I took it off a thousand times, this is stupid, am done! They can beat me up if they want to and you know why you only have one student? it is because you don't know Kung Fu" but what the karate kid later realized was that in routinely taking off and putting on his jacket he developed strong and quick hands and also swift mobility to bend down and get up, a series of dynamic movement that was crucial in Kung Fu. The karate kid just like most people who started off at something was obsessed with the outcome of his training, not the training itself, he wanted to be able to defend himself against bullies which was a good motivation but what he didn't expect was the amount of patience and dedication needed to practice the boring basics of Kung Fu. He wanted to dive straight into the interesting stuff and see his growth almost immediately just like most of us. But it was this forced dedication to the boring fundamentals that set him apart and made him a Kung Fu champion.

Floyd Mayweather will go down in the history of boxing as arguably the greatest boxer of all time with his official boxing record of 50-0. His success in the ring was not because he was physically stronger than his opponents a handful of his opponent were taller and had a better reach but if you had ever watched Mayweather in action you would see a fighter who has mastery over the basics of boxing. He knows how to move his head, how to shuffle his legs, how to lean backward and forwards, when to go in for a jab, and most importantly he knows when his opponent is hurt and when to go in for the kill. He is an all-round fighter and a true master of the game and it is no surprise that he has so much vastness in his locker since his father Mayweather Sr is a retired boxer and personal trainer.

Tyson Fury was also able to overcome a hard-punching Deontay wilder who dominated the heavyweight division for years with his powerful right hand in all of their three boxing matches not because he had more power but because he was an all-round fighter who was accustomed to the basics of boxing while wilder only relied on a powerful punch.

The truth is mastery of any craft is built on gruesome hours of *focused* purposeless practice of the fundamentals, a sense of purposelessness helps you not to focus on the result of practice but on the act of practicing itself so that you get lost in it and get the most out of it, with purposelessness mere practice turns into a form physical, mental and spiritual training. It gives integrity to the essence of practicing.

with mastery comes stillness, our mind is calm, and we do not feel the compulsive cognitive pressure that comes with focusing on results, deep within us there is a feeling of competency, our skills are so refined that we do not have to cognitively think to use them, even when there is a price to be won and the stakes are high you are, calm, compose and one with the present activity you don't think, you do. in sports, this state is referred to as being in the *zone*.

A perfect example of an athlete in the zone is Lionel Messi taking a free-kick of course he tries to bend it over the wall and place the ball in the net but there is not that much cognitive thinking, the technique for striking the ball is hard-wired in his mind that he doesn't have to think to execute it and most often he gets his desired outcome, this is due to total mastery of the act of kicking the ball that comes from endless hours of practicing the boring basics of football.

Just like the archer who when contending for a piece of earthenware seems to be more composed and skillful but when contending for an article of gold shoots as if he lost his skills so is it when we become obsessed with outcomes, we lose stillness and poise, our abilities and fortitude become hindered and we are unable to learn and develop properly. In Kenzo's school, it was when a student had fully detached themselves from the idea of hitting a target having spent months firing at a hay bale a few feet from them that he would finally announce "our new exercise is shooting at a target." And even when a student hits a target Kenzo will not shower the student with praise but urged them to continue practicing as if nothing has happened. He wanted them to get lost in the *process*

Have you ever noticed that the more you want something, the more insistent you are on a certain outcome and the more difficult it becomes to achieve it. The energy you spent aiming at the target is energy not spent developing your form. What we need in life is to be flexible, to be utterly present in the moment no matter how it may be, and to get to a place where there is nothing in our way including our own obsession with a particular outcome.

THE ILLUSION OF THE FUTURE

You have probably heard the saying *"the future does not exist"* but to put it in a plain and reasoning-provoking sense, the future is the natural proceed of the present moment whatever you could possibly become depends on the decision you are taking *now*. The reason you are who you are today is because of some of the decisions you made in the past. The level of your consciousness today will determine your future but most times we forget that the present is all we have, it is where our power lies, it is what is within our control and you should always try to make the most of it and not let imagined troubles steal it away from you. You have to form the habit of living in the present moment but it is most times very difficult due to the seldom ruthlessness of reality. You would rather escape from the present moment and obsess about the future and indulge in the habit of *connecting the dots* forward which then usually becomes depressing if there is an absence of a likelihood of

The desired outcome. We may reminisce about our past glories or involve ourselves in the illicit use of substances, anything to distract the mind from an underwhelming reality. This might bring momentary relief in the short term but it will become our own undoing in the long term.

instead of settling into the present moment and doing right by what we can control we instead become fortune tellers to ourselves and become anxious.
How will my life be a year from now? What do these imply for my children? Will I ever be happy again? Will my dreams ever become a reality? I hope they like me?

all of these questions are valid and important but they bother on prospects which are mostly outside of our control. Time spent pondering over them could be used to take tangible action. Be present you can cope with the future and you shouldn't bother yourself, if you take the right actions *now* the *future* will take care of itself. Fate will not favour you because you are worried but it might be benevolent towards you if you stand up and get yourself together and do right by what you can control with a knowing that no matter how brutal the reality of life might be as long you focus on what you can control and put in the work not allowing yourself to be crippled with anxiety and despair, you will prevail.

Concerning how we interact with the future I have classified human beings into three categories *the bad dreamer, the good dreamer, and the awakened.*

THE BAD DREAMER (the joyless robot)

When I was quite younger and obsessively ambitious about becoming a professional footballer, I generated a kind of toxic anxiety that never permitted me to actually enjoy living in the present moment, nothing really mattered not even my family. I will only become happy and be appreciative of my life when I sign that professional contract.

This then resulted in total dissatisfaction with who I was. As I grew older and felt my time was running out this feeling became even more intense. I could no longer celebrate birthdays, why should I be grateful for turning a year older when it only reduces my chances of making my dreams a reality. I was not grateful for a new month or new year neither did I participate in the whole *happy new month, happy new year* social media mania.

even the festivities and merriment at Christmas became trivial. I saw the passage of time as my enemy and there was this lame *willful* cognitive mental attempt to pause time, to stop time. Something that was totally out of my control *What height of madness!* and since I couldn't control fate certainly not in the way I went about it, I became a joyless robot. Only a professional contract will quench my agony.

At one point in our lives, we were bad dreamers especially when our dreams(ambitions) held our perceived happiness and freedom. The bad dreamer is so involved with the future that he neglects the present moment and what needs to be done to get where he wants to be. Bad dreamers are also bad learners, they are very obsessive and compulsive and lack the stillness and sobriety needed in mastering the *process*. He is delusional and out of touch with reality, the present moment is not lived in its full essence but is reduced to a stepping stone to the future. His whole life is based on hope, a bad dreamer is as happy as he is hopeful and so he is vulnerable to the twist and turns of fate, he is rigid in thinking and never far from anxiety, he is stuck in *trying to be*, he doesn't savour the present moment and changes around his life is invisible to him. a tree might grow and bear fruit right beside his house he might never notice it, he is locked in his head all day long with the present moment getting peripheral attention.

I was a bad dreamer a few years back before I had a rude awakening that I was wasting my life and was being less of myself because of an ideology, an ambition that I let define who I was and who I could ever be.

To sum up the experience a bad dreamer never truly live he exists in time.

THE GOOD DREAMER (the hopeful one)

My dad was a quintessence of a father and a husband. He was free-spirited, he loved his family, and he was hardworking and purposeful above all anybody who knew him knew that he was a visionary. He had his future planned out and he worked towards it. My fondest childhood memory of him was when we laid down on the mat under the moonlight and he would take the entire family on this illustrious journey into our glorious future, he inflamed me and my siblings with so much belief and enthusiasm about the future. His dreams were impressive and enchanting probably the reason I dreamt so hard myself. But unfortunately, my dad couldn't actualize his dream and died shortly after. My dad was a great dad he enjoyed the present moment, even though he was an ambitious man he still spends quality time with his family, an illustrious future was just something that kept his fire burning. majority of people are good dreamers, they savour the present moment, they are stable and mentally strong. They have a sense of gratitude and their happiness to an extent is not dependent on hope for a better future but they still prioritize the future over the present moment although this might help in taming them from taking reckless action that might hurt them in the future it still reduces the quality of their action and even a false absence of likelihood of a preferred future outcome might cause a great depression and a sense of purposelessness. Although the good dreamer savours the present moment he still sees it as a stepping stone to the future and doesn't fully live it to its fullest essence. He is motivated by hope and so vulnerable to the twist and turns of fate. It is very catastrophic for a good dreamer to lose hope because it is a primary motivator to live.

If fate plays his game, he would be the happiest person in the world if fate doesn't compromise, he might get depressed and give up. Although a good dreamer is more stable than a bad dreamer, he is more unlikely to become awakened, because for awakening to happen it requires a huge amount of suffering, one needs to get fed up but for a good dreamer, suffering is moderated so he never truly suffers until fate becomes too random. Most bad dreamers who go on the journey of self-development never get passed being good dreamers.

THE AWAKENED (the present one)

The awakened as the name implies literally means a person who is awake from his dreams. he is free of hope and fear. he is no longer dreaming and his dreams are nothing more than a guide, a guide that is not rigid but flexible. he is not focused or concerned about the future but grounded in the curiosity of the effect of his accumulated effort that it keeps him resilient and full of clarity even when the odds are against him. A perfect example of an awakened person was James Stockdale in Hanoi Hilton prison. Grounded, resilient, and full of clarity even in the face of great calamity.

An awakened person only focused on what is within their control in the present moment, no need to torment themselves with pointless concern about future events. His happiness is not based on hope for a future outcome, he understands that the purest form of happiness is peace and contentment with the present.

he is focused on mastering his craft with a knowing that *being* is a natural proceed of *doing*. Knowing that the future will one day be the present and the present moment was once the future. he understands that character is fate and pointless concern over the future will leave one weak and vulnerable. he is awakened because he is in touch with reality no matter how brutal it may be, he knows in the end he will prevail. For the awakened the journey is more important than the destination he takes one step at a time, he might be chasing a goal but he is also building a system. He is not trying to find, he is a creator, and nothing can happen to him everything is happening for him. he has mastered his craft so much that he is too good to be ignored, he is a perfect example of a craftsman. He is a joker the world is his playground nothing too important nothing unimportant, he is in one place at a time and has the mental discipline to carry his heart where ever he goes.

An awakened person is hardly agitated or anxious, he is calm, he doesn't seek validation he sees the opinion of others as something outside his control. He doesn't think too much he is in touch with the infinite possible and always in the flow state. He is never afraid to make a good mistake he sees it as part of the *process*. Failure only acts as feedback.

In my journey of self-development, it was my dissatisfaction and the enormous suffering that comes with trying to control what was outside my control that brought my awakening. I wouldn't even say I am an awakened person yet but it is something I try to work on every day of my life because to be awakened is to truly be in love with life and to truly live a meaningful life. a life that doesn't lack ambition but yet not enslaved by it. To be truly awakened is to know that you are bigger than your wildest dreams and if you pay close attention to the process not trying to skip any step you will prevail in the end no matter the outcome.

CONTROVERSY

The big takeaway here is not to live a life devoid of a dream or hope, if you don't have a vision for tomorrow how are you going to take the right steps in the present moment? The lesson here is to prioritize the actions you take in the present moment and be curious about the accumulated effect of those actions. this mentality will keep you grounded and give you clarity on the best action to take and what is more important. To be truly resilient in life we must focus on what we can control and we only have that power in the present moment not in the future or past.

LESSONS

1. Hope and fear are the flipsides of the same coin
2. To be resilient and persistent in life one must not focus on outcomes something that is outside their control but be curious about the effect of their accumulated effort over time, something within their control.
3. Fate won't favour you because you worry but it might be benevolent to you if you take the right action.
4. You don't achieve a dream by dreaming or by mere obsession but by being good at what is required of you, which requires a lot of present-moment concentration.
5. No matter the circumstance you find yourself, your freedom of choice cannot be taken away from you if you so wish.
6. Life is too short to be lost in a future inside our mind and be out of touch with reality.
7. Hope has a lot to do with the probability of things not happening.
8. Optimism is counterintuitive pessimism and vice versa
9. If you channel your energy and attention on the things which you control you will have clarity even in the face of calamity.

10.   To execute properly and achieve our target we need to let go of our cognitive willfulness to hit the target. We must learn to be purposelessly focused in other to achieve mastery.

CHAPTER TWO

DON'T BE YOUR *SELF*

Don't get into one form, adapt it and build your own and let it grow, be like water

Lao Tzu

But with me it is a very small thing that I be judge of you or of a man's judgement: yea I judge not my own self. For I know nothing against myself.

Paul the apostle

JESUS AND THE MONEYLENDERS

Jesus after turning water to wine at a wedding at Canaan which was recorded as his first-ever miracle in the bible, Jesus went into Jerusalem accompanied by his mother and disciples during the period of the Jewish Passover. When he went into the temple, he met a scene that made him furious. The Jews had converted the temple into a market, and they sold different merchandise most notably oxen and sheep. They were also exchanging money. If you had watched the movie or seen the clip of this scene on YouTube, you might have a better understanding of the amount of chaos Jesus single-handedly caused driving crowds of Jewish traders out of the temple. He outrageously poured away the money lender's money, turned over tables carrying their merchandise, opened the cages, and freed the animals. It was absolute chaos. speaking to those who sold doves he raged "take these things hence; make not my father's house a house of merchandise". for many Christians, this might seem a bit controversial and difficult to understand because Jesus is seen as a symbol of peace and serenity, someone who is harmless, and this is understandably so, due to his stance against violence in Mathew chapter five verse thirty-eighth to thirty-nine where he refuted the Jewish doctrine of an *eye for an eye* and *a tooth for a tooth* but instead admonish his followers to not put up a resistance against evil and if slapped on one side of the cheek they should turn the other "ye have heard that it hath been said, an eye for an eye and a tooth for a tooth. But I say unto you, that ye resist no evil, but whosoever shall smite thee on the right cheek, turn to him the other also"

For most Christians it will be nice to think Jesus was harmless and that he was incapable of violence but that is false. Jesus most often preached nonviolence and peace because they were major keys to sobriety and self-control which are doorways to surrendering to a higher power. When Jesus admonished his disciples to turn the other side of the cheek, he was not teaching harmlessness but self-control, avoiding the intense urge to retaliate which takes enormous strength, being in control of one's ego, and practicing virtue in the face of provocation. How can you believe in something greater than yourself when you are a slave to selfish impulses? Jesus didn't preach weakness but virtue.

The renowned author and clinical psychologist Jordan Peterson expatiated on the concept of being virtuous, in his words "if you are incapable of violence not being violent is not a virtue, the capacity for danger and the capacity for control is what brings about the virtue. Otherwise, you confuse weakness for moral virtue"

If you study the ministerial life of Jesus you notice he had a toolbox approach to his work on earth. He was not rigid in personality but camouflaged it in a way that was optimal in the present moment and also not against his values and purpose. He was more interested in *doing* than *being*.

To better navigate the world of men and bring salvation to mankind something he refers to as his father's business. In his divine wisdom he knew that to better execute his father's business in the ever-dynamic changing world he needed to be fluid in his personality and approach. Even in his humanness, he avoided the rigidity of the human ego.

When he came of age (30 years old) he went to the temple and declared himself as the son of God, this meant he was a sacred and holy being which he was, but he never protected this image. He associated with people who according to Jewish customs were the worst of sinners, these were the gentiles, prostitutes, and tax collectors, he respected some of the Jewish laws like payment of taxes "give what belongs to Ceaser to Ceaser and what belongs to God to God" and some he didn't respect such as being totally passive on the sabbath day even if it means starving to death " was man made for the sabbath or the sabbath for man" he preached nonviolence and peace but made an exceptions to these teaching when he violently drove money lenders out of the temple, he tried to break down scriptures for his disciples to understand yet he quizzed them with ambiguous parable. it was this fluidity in personality and approach and also the avoidance of the egoic rigidity that comes from being perceived as sacred that was responsible for the massive success of Christianity, it was definitely divine wisdom.

One of the major traits that were evident in the success of Jesus's ministerial work was his fluidity with his ego, he took his self-perception light-heartedly but his work heavy-heartedly. His actions showed he didn't really care about being perceived as sacred but instead showed his passion for his purpose which was to bring salvation to the world.

The truth is the *self* you know yourself to be is a social programming of your consciousness through the feedback of other people's perceptions and a knowing of your accumulated experience. In simple terms our personality is shaped by how we think other people think about us and our experiences in life (our known). For example, if a child made people laugh maybe through jokes or just with their mere demeanor, that child is going to grow up perceiving her *self* as a funny person and will tend to tell jokes more often or do things that causes laughter therefore, she will have a free-spirited and jovial personality. If that same child's life followed the opposite cause of events, she will take herself more seriously and sparingly try to be funny.

Our *egoic self* (self-perception/personality) is a social construct and was fabricated by external validation from the society. this is why we ought to take our *selves* light-heartedly and be recreational about it but keeping it in accordance with our values and sense of purpose. We should be forgiving of our past experiences and not let our *known* define us, be fluid in our thinking and avoid rigidity, be open-minded to learn new ideas, and be able to recreate and adapt our personality so that it is optimal in the present moment.

The lesson here is to avoid thinking in categories and fixed ideas which is mainly a result of social priming and life experiences (the known) but instead we should adopt a fluid approach to life.

Seeing the world in categories and separates limits our perception so we become stuck in our ideas of how things are supposed to be. As the universe is in constant flux and most things if not everything is more complex than our mind can comprehend, a more fruitful approach to life would be one that is flexible and enables us to flow along.

At my blog *zenfootball,* I try to teach most of my readers who are mostly young boys that are aspiring to become professional footballers that there many ways to become a professional and it is important to keep an open mind and to be fluid in how they approach this quest. In one of my articles titled *should I leave school to play football?* The core message was that if formal education happens to be part of your football journey then you should honour it, and find a way to combine school and football which in my opinion is not difficult, the top academies in the world like the *la masia* of Barcelona and *la fabrica* of Real Madrid function both as football and academic institution and also if schooling isn't part of your football journey it is okay. Then one of my readers contacted me on WhatsApp and told me he wished he came in contact with that article earlier as he had just dropped out of the university to pursue his dream of becoming a pro. first I asked him about his age, he was really young, then I proceeded to give him a little bit of advice, I told him for his age and the reality of the society we find ourselves the best approach to a pro career for him would be to combine football with formal education but since he already dropped out of school he should work twice as hard and improve his abilities to an impeccable level if he is to stand a chance and not regret his earlier decision. I was glad when he contacted me months later that he had gone back to the university and his footballing life had really blossomed. The fact is many professional footballers didn't go to the university while for some it was through tertiary education they got their opportunity, some were scouted from playing on the streets, a huge majority came through the football academy system, some sponsored themselves, traveling from city to city for trials till they got their big break and for some their dad owned a football club.

In life most people give up on their dreams or a course because they had a very rigid unidimensional approach to it. So, the moment their pre-planned route gets a backlash and loses the likelihood of taking them to the destination they seek they give up and abandon their quest instead of adopting a new approach.

How much more resilient will you be if you had a knowing that their many routes to the destination you seek. This is what Bruce lee meant in is his famous "be like water" speech. Water is the most resilient thing on earth, it cannot be obstructed neither can it be destroyed, if there is an obstacle along its path it flows around it, the obstacle does not become an obstruction but a guide. If you heat water it evaporates, if it finds itself in a cold environment it freezes to ice, if the ice is then kept at room temperature it melts into liquid water, when it is put into a container it takes the shape of the container. Water is truly resilient and cannot be inhibited because it is formless, always adapting and changing its form without losing its chemistry, it is optimal in the present, for water the obstacle becomes the way.

Just like water which is formless but maintains its basic chemistry we should adopt fluidity in our approach to life without losing our values or sense of purpose. It means we should take our ego lightheartedly and avoid rigidity in thinking so that we can flow better with our ever-changing world. The world is a playground but rigidity in thinking limits the experience and causes struggle.

Let's take an instance if you perceive yourself not to be funny and you develop an uptight personality that had benefited you in the past because people took you more seriously but you now find yourself in a cooperate work environment where you have a boss that is a joker and always loves a good laugh and you are also surrounded by colleagues with same jovial personality. You will flow better in that environment and have a better work experience if you adapt your personality and tell more jokes and "laugh it out" with your boss and colleagues without falling for the trap of the egoic narcissism of "being yourself". That doesn't mean you won't take your work seriously even if your colleagues have a lackadaisical approach towards work. The lesson here is to be fluid with your "self-perceived" uptight personality but stern in your values of always giving your best in whatever you do.

RE-INVENT YOUR *SELF*

Most times we create a narrative from our previous experiences (the known) in life that we force on every circumstance we encounter even when it is no longer optimal such that even past success becomes a hindrance to growth and a precursor for failure.

When Christiano Ronaldo signed for Manchester United in the summer of 2003 he was a blistering teenager of touch and tease, he was very a good dribbler and had his signature step-over move. It was these attributes that made him very successful in his first six years term at Manchester United, winning the premiere league, the champions league, and the most coveted individual award in football the balon d'or. When he signed for real Madrid in the summer of 2009 at the prime age of twenty-four, for ninety million euros and became the most expensive footballer in history. he reinvented his style of play, he no longer cared too much about dribbling past defenders but instead concerned himself with being an effective goal scorer. He sparingly did his signature stepovers instead he became more of a powerful shooter preferring to cut in from the wings and shoot at the goalpost. When he became thirty years old the beginning of an era where he will paradoxically score the most goals in his career.

He no longer concerned himself with most of the team play but instead played more in a central forward position, perfecting the timing of his run and movement inside the eighteen-yard box, he become a cutting-edge goal poacher. Any wonder why he won four more balon d'or and scored over seven hundred career goals becoming football all-time top scorer and arguably the greatest footballer of all time. Ronaldo's football success and longevity are due to the fact that he never relied on what made him successful in the past instead he adjusted his style of play to better match the energy his body could produce as he got older so that as-long he played his performance was optimal.

He aged like a fine wine. In his explosive interview with renowned journalist piers Morgan, Ronaldo talked about his adaptability "day by day we are getting old every one of us, you understand it is normal, you have to adapt and I think nobody in this game has this brain that adapts with his age, I am not going to be cocky to say that I am the same as I was when I was twenty, of course not, but I adapt and I am smart to know my strength and what am good at doing and I am still playing at the highest level scoring goals and I will continue to score goals if my mind is clear and I am happy"
Most player decline after thirty because they couldn't adapt their game, they get stuck to what they were doing in their twenties. It was after the age of thirty that Ronaldo's footballing prowess blossomed. As Ronaldo got older, he played simpler, he didn't try to dribble or outrun defenders like he did when he was eighteen instead, he became more intelligent with his movement on the pitch so that he could do the most important thing in football which is to score goals.

To achieve long-term success in life you must not allow the past to interfere with the present moment. Reduce past failure to lessons and past success to gratitude. You must be fluid and adapt to the demands of the present moment so that you are optimal in the present moment. Those who achieve long-term success have the humility to update their personality, they don't always force things to be done their own way because they know their own way might not be the best in every situation or might no longer be optimal. they quickly adjust and stay ahead. Ronaldo could have been himself and stuck religiously to his signature stepovers and flashy dribbles that brought him success earlier in his career and I could bet he wouldn't have experienced success as much as he did. He changed his style of play but not his work ethic.

THE LIGHT-HEARTED ACTIVITIST

Throughout history those who were regarded as greats had very fluid personalities and at one point in their life, they radically changed their perspective while unflinchingly standing for a course. Mohamed Ali is regarded as the greatest boxer of all time; he was an activist and fought against racial discrimination in the united states of America. His most charming attribute was his lightheartedness and sense of humor, these were not traditional personality trait for someone who is an activist and a fighter who needed to be taken seriously. Most fighters and activists settle rigidly into a hideous and stern personality in a bid to strike terror in the minds of their opponents but Ali instead did not settle for the stern traditional personality of a fighter or an activist. Although he was able to strike terror and was formidable in the eyes of his opponent, he remained fluid in his personality referring to himself as "pretty" and by displaying his immense sense of humor and wholesomeness on televised talk shows he become a public sweetheart.

Just like Mohamed Ali, Nelson Mandela was also a political activist. He formed a resistance group called "Umkhonto wesizwe" which translated to "spear of the nation" they violently revolted against the white-dominated apartheid South African government. He was convicted and sentenced to prison alongside his cohort in 1964 during his trials he made clear his unflinching resolution "I have cherished the ideal of a democratic and free society in which all persons live together in harmony and with equal opportunities. It is an ideal which I hope to live for and achieve, but if needs be it is an ideal for which I am prepared to die for" he spent the next twenty-seven years in captivity a period where he faced harsh treatment meant to break his resolve, he spent more than a decade breaking rocks. He was not granted permission to attend his mother's funeral in 1968 and the funeral of his son who died in a car accident in 1969. It would take him twenty-one years before he could hold his wife Winnie Mandela again. When he was released from prison in 1993 Mandela was still resilient in his fight for a free and equal South Africa but this time, he chose a peaceful approach, forgiving his oppressors, he negotiated an end to apartheid with the South African government and divorced his wife Winnie Mandela who had become an unrepentant violent anti-apartheid tyrant and whose actions had put the country on a brink of a civil war. Mandela's new approach worked, the South African government adopted an interim constitution that paved way for the country's first democratic elections, that same year he was awarded the Nobel peace prize award. In 1994 Mandela became South Africa's first democratically elected president.

Mandela's success came not as a result of abandoning the anti-apartheid movement but by adopting a new approach. Even though he suffered severe treatment in prison meant to suppress his resolution he never become a bitter person. During his public appearances just like Mohamed Ali he charmed his audience with his immense sense of humor.

FORGIVE YOUR *SELF*

Saul of Tarsus who later became known as Paul the apostle was a pharisee (Jewish lawmaker) who saw Christians as blasphemers and made it his life purpose to persecute them. He masterminded the persecutions of thousands of Christians in Jerusalem, his most famous victim was Stephen the deacon who he authorized his stoning to death. Because of his actions the Christians in Jerusalem lived in fear and most of them fled to Damascus and other neighboring cities. But Paul was far from done, he wanted to totally eradicate Christianity not only from Jerusalem but from all of Asia. He went to the high priest and received a letter of permission to go to Damascus to capture Christians and bring them bound to Jerusalem, it was on this journey to Damascus that he will encounter Christ and become a Christian and not just a Christian but he radically became a preacher of the gospel. Paul went on several missionary journeys planting churches all over Asia, on some of this expedition he would be imprisoned, on some he was stoned and his almost lifeless body was dragged outside the city, even his former pharisee colleagues plotted to kill him but this didn't deter Paul's new resolution. Paul's biggest challenge was not the calamity he faced as a result of his newly founded conviction but his history, the shadow of his former *self* hunted him, and the church and even some of the apostles were still very much wary of him. His former identity was fighting his integrity. In a letter to the Corinthian church Paul had to address the issue "but with me it is a very small thing that I should be judge of you, or a man's judgement. Yea I judge not my own self, for I know nothing against myself". Now let us take a look at another biblical figure Judas Iscariot. Judas was among the twelve disciples of Christ, a group of individuals which Jesus selected in his divine wisdom. He was also trusted to be in charge of the group's treasury but unfortunately for judas, he will have to play the role of betrayer in a divine prophecy. According to the bible an evil spirit possessed judas and he went on to betray his master in exchange for thirty pieces of silver. After the deed had been done, he came back to his senses and hanged himself to death.

If you compare the story of Paul and Judas you would notice the major difference is that Paul a persecutor and killer of Christians didn't identify with his former *self,* a self that was indoctrinated to see Christians as blasphemers but instead forgave that identity and became a preacher of the gospel while judas who was appointed to fulfill a divine mandate although not a glorious one, strongly identified with a betrayer *self,* a *self* that was possessed by an evil spirit so that even when he came to his senses which was then an opportunity to not only repent of his sin but also to forgive his self-perceived betrayer *self*. His rigid ego attachment didn't let him do that, instead he took the worst possible decision and killed himself.

The most important form of forgiveness is not being forgiven by others but forgiving one's own *self*. This is not only about forgiving yourself of your sins but also forgiving yourself for past failures, for the times you went depressed because things didn't go your way. It is about forgiving the suchness of the past and keying into the immense possibilities that abound in the present moment and in the future. It doesn't matter who you have been in the past or how hard your life had sucked, you can still become a better person, and you can still achieve success don't put your head down and take the worst but most comfortable decision. Paul persecuted and killed Christians, he never met Christ in person, only heard his voice from the clouds on his way to Damascus to cause havoc yet he was an instrumental figure in the propagation of Christianity, he planted most of the churches in ancient Asia and wrote fourteen out of the twenty-seven books of the new testament and he is today regarded as a saint while on the other hand judas was chosen by Christ as a disciple and entrusted with the treasury, he dined and wined with Christ and listened to all his teachings yet he became an uncelebrated figure in Christianity. Forgive your *self*!

THE FALSE HUMILITY`

I have a cousin named Caleb; I am a year older than him but it is a fact he finds difficult to come to terms with. Although we lived in different towns, we seldom visit each other during the holidays. Growing up as a kid we had a great relationship and we still do but there is always tension underneath the surface, due to the proximity of our age we competed for almost everything, we try so hard to outdo each other, and sometimes it gets toxic but it is something we both enjoy, we push each other to our limits. as kids we competed for who experienced puberty first and grew the most pubic hair, when we are opponent on the football field we try to dribble and mock each other, if we are playing a video game, we try to surpass each other's high score even when we sleep at night we fought for the blanket. I was older I was never going to allow him to outdo me and he relished every opportunity to do that. victory for the other person would lead to toxic trash-talking and mockery, we couldn't afford to lose to each other.

When I bought my laptop and installed pro evolution soccer (PES), it quickly became an avenue for our fierce rivalry, the battle for the ultimate bragging right. Unlike Caleb who grew up with video games and had a bunch of friends who had PlayStation, I didn't have a lot f video game experience but I had the willpower to avoid being humiliated on my laptop. Whenever we played PES, knowing that he was better I was always defending and he did most of the attacking. My game plan was to defend and counterattack through the wings then cross and try to get a header. a tactic I termed *cross and nod* It was the only feasible way I could score. It worked we drew almost every game we played and he never got that satisfaction of winning a streak of games.

Then on this faithful day, a day I will never forget in a hurry, he didn't only win all the games he tormented me with goals and violated my ego with the most creative trash-talk I have ever heard in my life, my self-esteem was saved by the electric power going off. We stopped playing around the time for our evening football practice and he asked to use my training boot. His demand for a grand favour after brutally destroying my ego was just a way of rubbing extra salt in my wound. I saw through it and I gave him nevertheless trying not to make my bitterness pathetic.

I had been humiliated, my ego was bruised and I needed a way to fight back or at least prevent such humiliation from ever occurring again. I spent the next two days avoiding Caleb, watching tutorial videos on YouTube, I set the PES to the highest difficulty and played against the games artificial intelligence practicing the tips I learned on YouTube. After gathering a little bit of confidence

I went back to playing with him. I changed my tactics I started trying to attack more, I wanted to play on the front foot, and I made peace with losing to him because I trusted the process. I knew I would change the narrative.

When we started playing, he won a chunk of the game as usual but I was beginning to enjoy the game more because I was no longer just defending, by this time he had exhausted himself with trash-talking. I just work hard and made sure I was practicing whenever we were not playing together. In subsequent days I began to win, and we began to share the number of wins. Whenever I won, instead of talking trash I kept my mouth shut.

In the coming days, I began to win majority of the games, and he started to give an excuse that his control pad was no longer functioning properly. Instead of making a mockery of him I showed empathy. In the subsequent days we would play throughout the night and he won't win a single game, I kept my mouth far away from insults and abuse. As I grew in confidence, I started using weaker teams and I was still able to win with a huge goal margin but instead of using that as an avenue to totally humiliate him with the greatest trash talk of all time, I showed empathy. There was a huge instinctive urge to totally ruin his self-esteem in revenge yet I did the opposite I made him feel comfortable being a loser. He started telling his friends about how good I had become; they will come to challenge me and I will destroy them and he would be in my corner cheering me up. I became a PES monster but I kept my ego under control.

There is nothing false about false humility I used the word *false* for the sake of expression, false humility is just humility with purpose. Many times, in life when we get a victory over a bitter rival we would instinctively give-in to the urge of *"in your face"* trash-talk. We enjoy that momentary satisfaction of humiliating that rival only for that rival to have the last laugh. Just like the proverbial hydra which grows an extra head when it is beheaded, we human beings have untapped potentials inside of us waiting for harm to be done to us. And since we can't harm ourselves, we rely on other people to do the job. If Caleb didn't make me feel as bad as I felt, I wouldn't had become as good as I became in PES. Armed with that knowledge I changed my approach I was not going to harm his ego; he is already better than me, and I don't want to be the guy that makes him unstoppable. So instead of emotional abuse I showed empathy, I made him a comfortable loser. Of course, even without my abuse he felt bad but not bad enough to awaken his untapped potential. I played the false humility; he is never use to me being humble so when I played the humility card he didn't know how to fight back or what to fight.

The truth is in life the greatest dose of motivation we can get are not from those that are in our corner but from our rivals. Because they are people who will do us harm or we perceive to be a danger to us and this keeps us on top of our game. The lesson here is if you want to be a serial winner for a long time you must learn to keep your ego under control not because you are afraid but because you want to be on top for a long time.

HEAL THE TROUBLED CHILD

Growing up as a child I was spontaneously radical, adventurous, and instinctively narcissistic. The kind of innocent selfishness that most children might showcase in refusing to share or give back a toy or a cookie. If you mix my childhood traits together, I will come-off as a very stubborn child. I was an outside baby; I was always on the street playing football or involved in an organized children street fight. I was never far from the chaos. I even earned the nickname *Bobo* due to my ruggedness. On one occasion my dad was shaving my elder brother's hair with a razor blade, I got angry because I wanted to go first, so I hit my dad's hand and he mistakenly cut my brother on the side of the face an incident that left a scar on his face. My behavior made my family to be wary of me especially my mum who was the family disciplinarian. I didn't grow up as a mummy's boy.

My mum did her best to tame me out of fear that it might be too late in the future, she put an end to my street name *Bobo*. She was never in my corner when something went wrong and I was involved, even if I was innocent although to be honest most times I wasn't. I was closer to my dad who was a free-spirited man, unlike my mum, my dad indulged me, and bought me a lot of toys, despite my inadequacies I felt I was his favourite kid. My elder brother and kid sister were the direct opposite of me calm, thoughtful, and most contrasting of all they were agreeable. I got a lot of sticks from my mum and my much older cousin brother who lived with us, my dad was my only solace. Growing up as a kid whenever my name was called at home, I will just think to myself "what have I done wrong again" my name was seldomly called for good and often times I would be found guilty. It was really traumatizing. If I got involved in a fight my mum wouldn't want to know the reason behind my provocation, it didn't matter if I was trying to protect myself, I would be disciplined nevertheless for fighting in the first place. My mum tried to tame me out of love and fear. She didn't want me to put her in conflict with other parents or grow up to be problematic to society but by doing this she over-intervened in my life and made me feel like a black sheep.

when I was eight years old my dad passed away. my only solace was gone. There was a huge shadow over his death because of how young he was, this was a bleak period for not just me but my entire family. We had to change town and my mum who resigned from her banking job a year before had to go back to the gruesome 9-5 banking life in order to take care of the family. My mum's banking job meant, we wouldn't have any parental presence in a new town where we were strangers, this terrified not just my mum but me and my siblings. My worldview changed I became very scared of life. Since my mum was mostly not going to be present parenting became more psychological than physical. The free time she had on Saturday morning were used to remind us how cruel the world could be and to admonish us to thread carefully and stay out of trouble, to always turn the other cheek even in face of unacceptable provocations especially now that we are fatherless and since she is now always busy with work she wouldn't cope well with any extra troubles. It was this psychological priming that finally broke me.

So, I grew up scared and anxious at the same time filled with anger. since my fondest childhood memories were made with my dad, a part of me refused to grow up. Even as I became an adult, I still had that childish *self* that wouldn't come to terms with reality, I wanted things to be as it was in past or in the glorious future my dad promised me, this was amongst the reasons I became a *bad dreamer* because a part of me was stuck in psychological time.

Due to being treated as the problem child I unconsciously bought into the idea that I was a problem, this limited the amount of confidence I had in myself, I self-sabotage whenever things didn't go my way, I sought outside validation so badly, people's opinion were paramount, even when I was wronged, I was afraid to stand up for myself and I will then turn that aggression against myself. I tried so hard not to fit into the stereotype of being a problem child that I wasn't expressive of my true feelings and accumulated a lot of anger which eventually violently spiraled out of control to reinforce that stereotype. I developed a huge sense of entitlement, I felt because my dad died the world owed me something this affected the way I took responsibility for my life. It was when my suffering became unbearable which came as a result of opposing reality and having a rigid ego identity that didn't flow well with life, that I got my rude awakening. I knew I was not living right and was at risk of living a sad life. I wanted to love life again so I started to seek help. I watched a lot of self-help videos on YouTube, read a lot of self-help books, listened to a lot of podcasts, I did anything to elevate my mind. With the knowledge I gained I was able to change a lot of my physical and mental habits, I started practicing meditation and I became more aware of my thought pattern. As I continued my self-development journey, I became more self-aware and realized there was a part of my egoic *self* that needed to heal. The only way I was ever going to heal was to change the narrative in my head, I needed to tell my *self* a different story. I told my *self* that everything that happened in my life was for good and it is also my responsibility to make it good. It was time to forgive the past and accept the reality of the present moment. Ever since then I have approached my life with a sense of responsibility and I noticed I became happier and less worried. I began to fall in love with life again.

Our perception of the world is majorly shaped at childhood by society, memorable events, and most fundamentally by our parents or guardians. If you had parents that indulged you, you might grow up confident and reckless, if you had an overbearing disciplinarian parent you might grow up to be well-behaved and responsible but lacking in confidence. The truth is our parents tried to raise us the best way they could but by doing this they most times over intervened in our life. This over-intervention could be by being overly protective of a child that she is not allowed to go outside to play on the streets with fellow kids in a bid to protect her from an imaginary danger that she grows up being rebellious and naïve. shaming a child to get a rise out of them that they grow up to be fierce competitors but lacking in compassion, parents being too caring that they never allow their children to do anything by themselves that they grow up feeling incompetent, in doubt of their abilities and dependent. the list could go on and on.

We might not all grow up with trauma but we all have our different insecurities, anxieties, and phobias. To solve this issue, you have to connect the dots backward to where it first started so that you can understand the root of your psychological priming, why you behave the way you do, and what triggers those unwanted behaviours. Armed with this awareness you can deconstruct those hard-wired psychological beliefs and build a new thought pattern, the new *self*.

This chapter is filled with religious undertone, because that is the essence of religion, believing in a higher power, something higher than the *self*. something that anchors us and gives us a sense of value at the same time frees us from the tyranny of our egoic *self*. This was why Jesus knew when to put his foot down and when to turn the other cheek, this was why a repented Paul even after persecuting thousands of Christians knew nothing against his *self*, it was the reason why I was able to heal the troubled child. With a belief in something higher than our self we can avoid a strong ego identity and flow better with life.

By seeing our personality(self) as a tool not us, we won't fall for selfish impulses and we would build self-control, we won't get offended by insults or take other people's inadequacies personally because we will not have a personality to be attacked. Having a fluid personality means you would never go out of options and will be more resilient, most importantly you will be optimal in the present moment, adapting, growing, reinventing, and being unstoppable.

CONTROVERSY

Despite having a fluid personality, we should have rigid values (moral ethics) that we uphold or we risk being hypocrites. Values are very important because they help in shaping and giving meaning to our life. If human beings lived without ethics the world would be much more chaotic. Although we can always change our values, it should be done after a thorough examination of what is fundamentally true or false. Jesus upheld some Jewish values like payment of taxes but others he didn't like being totally passive on the sabbath day that you risk starving to death.

Think of value as a compass, a general direction to a destination then think of personality as a map, a pre-planned route.

To get to our destination in life, our values are the compass that shows us the direction to go, in that direction, there are many routs(personality) we can take to get to our destination. We can choose any route convenient or change to a more convenient route as long as it is in the direction of the compass. The moment we become solely attached to a particular route we become vulnerable to limitations. If there is a blockage or a wild animal along that route our journey becomes stunted and we won't be able to reach our destination. Also, you can choose to totally change your direction and seek another destination but if you are still not fluid in your approach you might still find yourself changing your direction towards another destination instead of just changing your route. Fluidity in approach protects the rigidity of our resolution.

LESSONS

1. True virtue lies in self-control, not harmlessness
2. Have a toolbox approach to anything you do in life, you would be more resilient if you are open to other options
3. Don't be your *self* instead be optimal in the present moment
4. Be careful with the story you tell your *self* so that you don't get casted into a rigid narrative and waste your life protecting an image.
5. Be open to learning and adapting to new ideas, what brought success in the past might no longer be optimal.
6. Forgive the past whatever happened in your life was for your good and it is your responsibility to make it good.
7. Be unpredictable, do not allow your rival to figure you out, learn to play multiple personality cards.
8. Values can also change but should change after a thorough examination of what is false and what is true.
9. The egoic self is a product of social programming, don't get casted into a rigid ego-identity instead be fluid with your personality but rigid with your values (moral ethics)
10. Love yourself

CHAPTER THREE

DON'T FOLLOW PASSION

Man should not live by a single hope

Seneca

The key to living a happy work life is not in doing what you love but in loving what you do.

Calvin Newport

THE CATSKILL MONASTERY

Cal Newport's eye-opening book *be so good they can't ignore you* it begins with the fascinating story of Thomas who after earning a pair of bachelor's degrees in philosophy and theology then a master's degree in comparative religion was obsessed with being a full-time practitioner of Zen Buddhism. It was his passion. Thomas decided that Zen Buddhist practice was the key to him living a happy life, so he decided he would become a monk. After his graduation from school Thomas needed money to chase his dream and money was not going to stop him. he worked a couple of menial jobs and was able to finance his ambition. He got admission into the Catskill Zen mountain monastery. On his arrival at the monastery gate, he was buzzing with excitement and enthusiasm this was where his passion told him he belonged, he was about to be the most fulfilled man on earth. He had mustered the courage to follow his daydreams and had made them a reality. At the beginning of his journey as a monk, he was intrigued by teachings and practices of Zen Buddhism but as time passed when he reached the zenith of his passion and had become a full fledge Zen practitioner, he came to a shocking but inevitable realization that Zen Buddhism was not as enterprising as his passion had told him, it didn't meet the expectation his daydreams fantasized about.

His anxieties and worries did not go away, he didn't change from who he was, and the enthusiasm and excitement that had accompanied him on his arrival at the monastery gate were nowhere to be found, this realization brought Thomas great depression.

Thomas followed his passion to the Zen mountain believing as modern-day motivational speakers preach that the key to a happy life lies in identifying one's true calling and following it with all the courage one can muster but Thomas realized the path to happiness as it concerns what you do for a living is much more complex than simply answering the classic question *"what should I do with my life"*

I have always suspected that passion is not as mystical or monogamous as modern-day conventions try to preach and it was when I came in contact with Cal Newport's eye-opening book that I gained clarity. passion is nothing more than terms and conditions being met. At the base of these terms and conditions is the quest for *control*. The freedom to do what we like, when we like, and how we like. If you think retrospectively about the things you are passionate about you are really good at them and you have practiced the required skills for a long period, you don't need instructions or other people's intervention to do it, you feel a deep sense of freedom when you engage in those activities this might create an eagerness to find a work that matches your passion. This is also partly because we have this modern-day false indoctrination that we can escape the rigorousness of work in active life. A kind of work that we will never have to work a day in our life. this obsession to escape work has become the cash-cow for online entrepreneurs, many times I have come across very ridiculous adverts on social media such as *became an author without writing a book, get admission even if you don't have a JAMB result, go to heaven without having to die.* The last one was a bit of an exaggeration but you get my point. This obsession to match our careers to passion in a bid to escape work builds a sense of entitlement, expectation, and disregard for responsibility. It sets us on an endless pursuit to seek purpose in external things and it takes away our power to create our own purpose this results in doubt and a pathetic work life.

We live at a time where the glory of passion is at an all-time high, it is very hard to watch an award show that the winners didn't attribute their success to finding their purpose and chasing it will all the courage they could muster in a bid to sound motivational. This continues to ignite the purpose finding passion-centric mindset that is now the norm of our modern world, it is so satisfying and mysterious that we don't fact-check its relevance or study the behind-the-scenes of our career idol's life to observe how certain and precise they were about their purpose and whether it was this unflinching obsession to this precisely chosen purpose that helped build the compelling career that they love and it is been envied by you and millions of people. If you ever did this behind-the-scenes research you would realize that the famous motivational award soundbite *follow your passion* is not a particularly useful advice, it is only good for the media because it is vague, lack useful details and breeds doubt and confusion. What you would realize is that what our career idols have managed to become had nothing to do with *the certainty* that they had found their purpose and completely dedicated their life to that course instead you would realize a more *tentative* approach.

The compelling careers of our career idols were built on the foundation of years of acquiring rare and valuable skills known as *career capital* in multiple career endeavors through years of brute hard work and deliberate practice and then making little bets at different endeavors to see what works and what doesn't and then cashing in this *career capital* where there is an opening from a bet that worked.

THE PASSION OF LINDA IKEJI.

The most compelling careers are the ones that guarantee control over time and give financial freedom. The freedom that comes with being the boss of oneself and having all the money to engage in one's fantasies are precursors for living a passionate work life. Linda ikeji the Nigerian billionaire blogger fits into the category of those who have made a compelling career and are living the dream life. As a writer and a blogger, Linda Ikeji is the perfect career idol for me, her blogging career has been nothing short of exceptional. If there was anybody, I was going to research the importance of knowing one's purpose and chasing it with all the courage one can muster as a pre-requisite for achieving a compelling career should be my career idol.

As I started my quest, I came across a five-year-old video on a YouTube channel named Lindaikeji TV. The video was titled *Linda ikeji's message to every young girl out there.* As it is customary of modern-day public figures, they try to be role models in society and if they happen to be women it is a role they wouldn't take lightly. The video starts with a quote from Steve maraboli that says *"the empowered woman is powerful beyond measure and beautiful beyond description"* then it was followed by a piece of cinematic music that solemnly introduced Linda into the scene, the background was totally blacked out which blended with her black wig, her face was the most colourful thing in the scene it was as if she was the light in the darkness. Her message was to young girls urging them not to follow the wayward life of becoming sex workers as a means to earn a living, something along the line of not allowing men to take away their dignity for the sake of money, a classic advice for women since the beginning of time. She also emphasized the freedom that comes with making fortune on one's own terms and living an independent life and that this freedom is achievable if they have the drive and determination to work hard.

She narrated her failures and struggles in her quest to build a compelling career "some days I would lay on my bed and I would cry my eyes out and I would get up work, fail and then I would cry some more" towards the end of her video as it is customary of all motivational video the best motivational soundbite is kept for the end. In her final words she said "find your purpose believe in your purpose, live your purpose"

It was a very inspiring and motivational message one that supports the idea that great careers are built on finding a work that one is passionate about (purpose). But let's do a quick behind the scene career research on Linda ikeji. The world knows Linda as a successful blogger but if you were a close friend or relative to Linda before her blog gained traction in 2011, you will know for a fact that she always wanted to be a model, she had so much passion for pageantry, it was the dream that kept her awake at night. She started her modeling career at the young age of seventeen just after completing her secondary education. She enrolled at the University of Lagos at the age of eighteen where she continued her modeling career. To testify to how passionate she was about modeling she organized the miss university of Lagos pageantry for three consecutive years, in 2003 she contested Miss Nigeria. After finishing her tertiary education, she started her own modeling and event company which failed because of lack of proper financing. She started a magazine it also didn't blossom; she started a marketing and PR company which also became a failure, she attempted to start a reality TV modeling competition it never became

a reality. She organized an annual fashion show for seven years it didn't produce any tangible profit; she wrote a book and didn't sell up to five hundred copies. In her own words "thirteen years after starting my hustle I was still broke and struggling"
As you may have noticed these are not the footprint of someone who had the certainty of a specific purpose or passion and chased it but of someone who had a resilient tentative approach to work life. On a deeper level she understood that purpose is vague and open-ended and she could create her own purpose if one of her little bets hits the jackpot of a compelling career.

You may have also noticed that there has been no mention of her blogging. This is because her blogging career was the least of all her tentative bets. This is understandably so because she didn't grow up during the internet age, she was born in the early 1980s in eastern Nigeria and had no childhood dream that the internet held her fortune. She started blogging as a hobby later in her adult life in the early 2000s a period that marked the beginning of the internet age in Nigeria. I wonder who blogs as a hubby in a period where internet facilities and computers were very scarce but if you have been paying attention this was just another one of her career bets. One that she didn't even take as seriously as the others "before I had my breakthrough in blogging, I blogged for four years without making any money, those days I will beg for 100 naira to pay for browsing time at the cybercafé, but then in 2011 everything changed, companies started paying me for something I had nurtured with love"

Between 2011 to 2017 which is an interval of six years her blog boomed and Linda ikeji became a household name. she was the first to ever reach that height in mainstream media as it concerns blogging in Nigeria. by the time she made her motivational video in 2017 she boosted of acquiring a house worth over 750 million naira ($1,657,128.9) and a car valued at 70 million naira ($154,665.37)

Did Linda ikeji find her purpose? Or her purpose found her when companies started paying her to advertise on her blog? the truth is a sense of purpose doesn't totally depend on money but on value (usefulness) but money is a potent neutral indicator of value.

Linda ikeji didn't become an exceptional blogger because she was passionate about writing on the internet or because she knew with utmost specificity that blogging was her purpose and dedicate her life to it. It was less dramatic and mystical than that. Her blogging career started as a result of a lucky break, a small-time scheme that unexpectedly took off, I do not doubt that Linda eventually grew passionate about her work but all that tells us is that "it is good to enjoy what you do" what Linda ikeji has taught us is that the classic advice "follow your passion" is not a particularly useful advice and also the classical question "what should I do with my life" cannot be narrowed down to specificity.

THE TRAITS OF A COMPELLING CAREER: TERMS AND CONDITIONS FOR PASSION.

According to scientific studies of workplace motivation which is summarized in a theoretical framework known as the self-determination theory (SDT). which is currently the best scientific understanding for motivation.

The SDT proposed that motivation in the workplace or elsewhere requires the fulfillment of three basic psychological needs which are required for a person to feel intrinsically motivated for work. They are;

1. **AUTONOMY:** the feeling that you have control over what you do and how you do it and also control over your time.

2. **COMPETENCE:** the feeling that you are good at what you do

3. **RELATEDNESS:** the feeling of connection with other people, that your work can impact people's life positively.

The last one is the most obvious if you enjoy the company of your colleagues at work you are definitely going to enjoy doing your work. Also, the more you become better at what you do especially if you stand out amongst your colleagues you are definitely going to get preferential treatment with this treatment comes control and a great feeling of competence. When these three psychological factors are met even in the worst job on earth a person is bound to be passionate.

PASSION IS A NATURAL PROCEED OF MASTERY

Growing up in suburban Nigeria I was used to playing a football five-aside game known as *set*. set is played between three or more teams at the end of a set time the winner continues to play while the loser goes out for another team(set) to come in. the most important criterion for success in a set game was having the best legs on your team, with a good team a set can play from kickoff till it gets dark. I was one of the best players in my neighbourhood at the time and I was a hot catch, I could single-handedly guarantee my set success. I was so good because I was almost always playing football not out of hard work but for leisure, my dad was a huge football fan and always bought me a ball anytime I anytime I demanded for one but some of the other kids had very strict parents who preferred their kids to remain indoors and study during their free time. Whenever they manage to escape the prison walls of their home to play football on street their inferior skill-set made people like me outstanding. My rare and valuable football skills earned me a lot of preferential treatment that kept my passion blazing. I could afford to come out late and still have teams fighting to have me in their set, this was a huge privilege considering the fact that the set system was organized to remedy overpopulation and make sure everybody participates, some kids can't afford to come out late or they risk being spectators but not me I was different, I was special. Because my abilities were superior to most of my peers, I felt a sense of competence and most of the kids I played with regularly especially those who were regularly my *set*-mate became my close friends.

If you think retrospectively about all the things you are passionate about as it relates to a hobby you are very good at them your skills are so refined that you do those things effortlessly and if you have good self -awareness you will notice that the better you got at those activities the more you love to indulge in them also on the other hand the things you are not passionate about are the things you struggle to do and they make you feel miserable. This points to two facts, the first is passion is a product of *mastery* and secondly mastery takes time. this proves that being passionate or feeling a deep sense of purpose is not a one-way thing neither is it set in stone but instead, it shows that you can develop passion or a sense of purpose in any life endeavor as long you have the tenacity to show up every day till you acquire *mastery* and then trade the career capital (rare and valuable skills) you have acquired in your quest for mastery for traits that make a career compelling which will then result in you being passionate about your work

THE FLAW: WHY *"FOLLOW YOUR PASSION"* MIGHT BE A DANGEROUS ADVICE

In 2002 a research team led by Canadian psychologist Robert Vallerand administered an extensive questionnaire to a group of five hundred and thirty-nine Canadian university students. The questionnaire prompts were designed to answer two important questions, do these students believe in passion? and if so, what are they? When the results of the experiment were compiled, 84% of the student surveyed were identified as having passion, on taking a deeper dive into the details of their pursuit the top five identified passion were dance, reading, swimming and hockey. Though dear to the heart of this students these passions don't have much to offer in terms of a career. Most people in the world have these types of recreational passions that lack or have very slim work applications.

For these Canadian students, a vast majority will need a different approach to a career.

Even if you are among the fortunate few who manage to get a job that matches their passion, your huge expectation of what a dream job should be put you at risk of disappointment and even hating your work. The passion-centric mindset is more concerned with the traits of a compelling career such as *control* that it paralyzes a person's sense of responsibility towards work but the traits that make great work compelling takes time and require patience and hard work to acquire enough *career capital* (rare and valuable skills) to trade in exchange for them. The passion hypothesis in lay terms states that for you to be happy with work-life you have to match work with your expectation of work. It is indirectly asking you, does this work match your daydreams? If *yes* you can be happy now if *no* you can choose between being unhappy or being unstable. The latter is where most people find themselves jumping from one endeavor to another searching for a sense of purpose and fulfillment
For instance, if your passion is reading and you get employed in a book reviewing company that requires you to read a certain number of books and give your reviews within a limited amount of time let's say two books per week, do you think you will enjoy the same amount of control you enjoyed

when you just read books for leisure and could finish it anytime you want? Definitely not! Nobody is going to pay you to play by your rules and even if you are a freelance book reviewer your deadline to some extent still takes away your autonomy. What this means is that as far as we choose to work irrespective of the work we do. we can't escape the regiment of work and we should be okay with that. If you expect the same amount of enjoyment you felt when you read for leisure from your professional book reviewing job you may end up hating your work and seeking another endeavour. What this teaches us is that passion can be fleeting, it is a psychological reward that is present when the traits of great work are present and it is absent when these traits are absent. To approach work with passion-driven expectation is to become vulnerable to misery during periods where work doesn't provide those traits, especially during the early periods when you have not achieved mastery.

Passion gives away our sense of fulfillment to things outside of our control like our work. It set our mind on what our work can offer us like financial freedom(control), how people will perceive us (respect) and how much of an impact we can have but it disregards responsibility, what can we offer? The part we need to play. The Passion hypothesis tells you to be happy when work meets your expectations, which work may never meet especially with a high sense of entitlement and no value to give in return. The conventional advice *Follow your passion* might be a catalyst for instability and unhappiness in life.

THE PASSION OF LADI

My mum had worked as a banker all her life working life. She gave birth to me while working for the bank and I grew up knowing my mum as a banker until 2007 when she decided she was tired of the 9-5 cubicle-dwelling banking lifestyle. The banking job looks very fanciful from the outside because bankers get to dress smartly to work and for some understandable reasons people think bankers have all the money in the world but those who are in the system especially in a third-world country like Nigeria are always job hunting during their free time.

Banking job is the typical 9-5 job that the *courage culture* of the modern world admonishes people to quit. The comical truth is banking job is not even a 9-5 job it is more of a 7-10 job as I had observed in my mum's banking career. Back to our story, my mum has had enough of the regimented banking life and in 2007 she resigned and started an agricultural business where she buys produce in wholesale and resell in retail. She was finally free to live her life on her own terms and now has the time to stay close to her family but little did she know that a black-swan event was right around the corner which would make her freedom short-lived. the following year my dad passed on leaving behind a very young family that comprised of my mum, my elder brother, my two younger sisters and myself.

We had to change town to start a new life. Without the support of my dad and months of mourning and moving around my mum couldn't continue her agriculture business and it was only a matter of time before our lack of income begins to take a toll on us. So, my mum had to go back to the constricting and time-regimented banking job that gave her a breath of fresh air when she resigned some months ago.

You might think it should be much easier to work in the bank now since she had previous experience instead it was the opposite. It was more like being stuck in a job you do not want to do but you no longer have a choice because you have four kids to carter for.

In her second spell in the bank, she started off as a contract staff that is a temporal staff that could be laid off at any time. she worked as a cashier, which is the most tedious and mental health wrenching position in the bank. The cashiers are at the bottom of the banking food chain. They do the most work because they are in charge of all physical cash transactions with a very minimalistic salary. Most times about a quarter of that salary is used to pay back shortages incurred when they mistakenly overpay customers and were unable to balance the books.

In the early stages of her second spell, my cashier mum will come home late in the night sometimes as late as 11 pm often times I would wake up to see her the next morning preparing to go back to work. Other times I would wake to her sobbing in the middle of the night, she had a shortage the previous day which will be deducted from her salary by the end of the month. Coupled with the fact that she recently got widowed with four children, tears were never far from her eyes. The next morning up she goes, as early as the morning bird.

She always went to work on time and gave it her best although it didn't insulate her from the seldom setbacks of shortages nevertheless, she was relentless and full of work ethic.

It didn't take long before my mum's pragmatic approach to work yielded dividends. She was among the few temporal staff out of many who got promoted and made a permanent staff of the bank with that came a salary that tripled her previous earnings, she was moved from the counter and made a customer service officer a position where active work ends by 4pm and she got to be involved in important banking delegation, she also got the chance to interact and build relationships with customers.

This new position gave her more *control* over her time since active work ends by 4pm, she could come home as early as 7 pm. the salary increase brought a bit of financial freedom she could now start her own project. Being involved in crucial banking decisions gave her a sense of *competence* and *impact*. She could relax a bit more to catch a gist with fellow colleagues and customers.

By the time my mum left the bank in the early parts of 2022, she had risen to the post of a business service manager which is one of the two most senior positions a banker can hold within a bank branch. She was in charge of all business operations in the bank, she could come home as early as 6pm, and she could now postpone her task till the next day if it became overwhelming. She could send her junior colleagues who now look up to her as a role model to run personal errands for her, major banking decisions now depended on her, due to her relationship with customers over the years some of them became family friends and were more than happy to gift my mum their farm produce, tip her money and other incentives even if at that point in her career she didn't really need them. She became a mother figure within the bank, a role model especially for the younger women.

My mum was no longer coming home exhausted or crying late at night, it wasn't hard to tell that she found purpose in being a banker, her blazing passion couldn't go unnoticed.

By the time she resigned she had managed to see me and my elder brother through our tertiary education, built her own house, bought a good car and raised a chunk of foster children. She also had enough money to start her own business.

The truth is that my mum's career path is the most realistic prototype of work life, you start at the bottom then you work your way up. The guys at the top have stayed around long enough to achieve mastery and see the impact of their job on the world hence are more passionate and feel a deep sense of purpose than the guys at the bottom who just started their career journey. If you just started your job it is normal to not feel passionate as you would have imagined but if you stay long enough and put in the work ethic needed to achieve mastery you will be able to turn that job into a compelling career that you will truly be passionate about and feel a deep sense of purpose. My mum could have been unhappy or unstable instead she chose patience and accepted responsibility and built a career that in retrospect she wouldn't trade.

THE CRAFTSMAN

If following your passion as a prerequisite for a happy work life is a wrong advice then what is the right approach to work?
This is where the craftsman hypothesis comes in it states that the traits of great work that keep the fire of passion burning are rare and valuable and if you want these traits in your working life you must possess rare and valuable skills also known as *career capital* to trade. This career capital (rare and valuable skills) serves as a currency in purchasing the traits that breed passion. The craftsman mindset preaches that "working right trumps finding the right work"

When you look at the story of billionaire blogger Linda ikeji, her years of failure as a model, an event manager, an author and a failed TV show were not actually failures. All this time that her various endeavors didn't blossom she was receiving feedback on what worked and what didn't work. She was acquiring career capital in the showbiz business and by the time her blog blossomed she already knew how to craft the perfect headlines; she knew what was newsworthy and what was not newsworthy. Linda was not the first blogger in Nigeria nor was she the only blogger at that time but she was the only blogger with that vast amount of career capital.

ACQUIRING CAREER CAPITAL

To become a craftsman and set yourself apart from the competition, it entails *becoming so good that you can't be ignored.* First, you must acquire rare and valuable skills (career capital). You acquire career capital by intentionally stretching your abilities beyond your comfort zone and then receiving immediate feedback this process is termed *deliberate practice.* It implies pushing yourself beyond your limit, making your practice Intentionally difficult and intensive and then receiving vital feedback on your progress.

Many people especially those who don't want to take responsibility but want all the traits of a great work avoid deliberate practice because it requires brute hard work both physically and mentally. It also requires persistence, patience and being okay with the criticism of your abilities (feedback).

Feedback can come from a trainer or coach, from results and efficiency of approach (what worked and what didn't). feedback can be a gentle pat on the shoulder followed by a piece of fatherly advice but in most cases, feedbacks are brutal and displeasing. For Linda ikeji feedback came as re-occurring failures, for a footballer it could be sitting on the bench and watching others play, for my mum it came in the form of shortages. For an entrepreneur who just a started business feedback could be poor sales but feedback can also be good if you succeed at something it must mean you did something right. The aim of displeasing feedbacks is not to stampede your growth or frustrate you but to set you up for success, to show you your weaknesses, in summary the aim of feedback is to teach you what works and what doesn't so that you can continue tweaking your approach and getting better.

Deliberate practice requires a lot of hard work, consistency and being open to criticism which is why many people don't indulge in it. What most people do is that they practice their skill to an acceptable level of good then they get relaxed and refuse to push themselves past that limit, their abilities plateau and they become average, not bad but not extraordinary, just good.

A craftsman is never okay with being average, wherever he finds himself he is not satisfied with being part of the system but being the system. A perfect example of a craftsman is Christiano Ronaldo even at the age of thirty-seven and playing for a massive club like Manchester united, he wasn't satisfied with being a squad player. He is either the main man or nothing else.

A craft man is never afraid of leaving their comfort zone, they practice and practice with subsequent training becoming more challenging. He is okay with receiving ruthless feedback. He acquires rare and valuable skills (career capital) that distinguish him from his contemporaries he then trades his career capital for the traits that turns work into a compelling career and so he is even more passionate.

THE 10,000-HOUR RULE

The ten-thousand-hour rule states that for a person to achieve mastery in performing a complex task, it will take that person ten thousand hours of practice which is about ten years. The ten-thousand-hour rule came as a result of psychologist studying chess players to determine the hours of practice required to become a grand master. It was then popularized by the author Malcom Gladwell in his 2008 best-selling book *outliers*. In the outliers, Malcom pointed out this rule as evidence that great individual accomplishments are not about natural talent but instead it is about being in the right place at the right time to accumulate a massive amount of practice.

In the outliers, a group of violinists were divided into three groups according to their level of ability. The *teacher material, the good,* and the *world-class* then they were all asked the same question ever since you pick the violin how many hours of practice have you given to it?

A pattern emerged the teacher material had practiced for about four thousand hours, good had practiced for about eight thousand hours and world-class had practiced about ten thousand hours. Study after study with pianists, chess players and con artists produce the same pattern. The outliers pointed to this conclusion, as long as you are good enough what will separate you from your competitors is the number of deliberate hours of practice you put into your craft.

The ten-thousand-hour rule holds three major lessons;

1. When you are in your first few hours of doing something do not expect to be good and judge yourself by other people's standards especially those who started before you. You are probably going to suck at first and receive displeasing feedbacks which would help you get better

2. Talent is overrated and it proceeds from accumulating hours of practice. I can relate to this because I have been put on that pedestal in the past, going back to my childhood days of playing football(soccer) on the streets my peer saw me as a football demigod but my superior footballing abilities were not because of an innate congenital talent but because of

the amount of time I spent practicing with my personal ball.

3. Thirdly it teaches that as long as you are good enough deliberate practice is what will set you apart. It is not the number of hours put into practice that is the differentiating factor but how deliberately those hours are being used. You could practice your craft heartedly for ten thousand hours and you still won't be outstanding and won't match the abilities of someone who has been deliberate about their ten thousand hours of practice.

THE CRAFTSMANSHIP OF TIGER WOODS

Anyone who knows a thing or two about golf is not oblivious to the greatness of tiger woods and the impact he has had on the sport. Tiger became a professional golfer in 1996 at the age of twenty and by April 1997 he had won three PGA tour events and a masters which he won by twelve strokes in a record-breaking performance, he also reached number one in the world ranking in 1997 just less than a year of turning pro.

Tiger woods dominated golf in the first decade of the twenty-first century, he was the top ranked golfer in the world from August 1999 to September 2004(264consecutive weeks) and again from June 2005 to October 2010 (281 consecutive weeks) during this period he won thirteen major golf championship. Four masters, four PGA championships, and three US open championships. He was also PGA player of the year for eleven inconsecutive years and holds the record for most PGA tour wins with eighty-two wins.

It is not in doubt that tiger is one of the greatest golfers that ever lived. On the surface his golfing exploits could be attributed to talent and following his passion considering the fact that he was a child prodigy and truly showed his passion on the golf course but on a deeper dive into tiger woods early life you would discover that his exploits were nothing short of gruesome craftmanship.

The seeds of tiger's exploits were sown early, his father Earl woods was a very complicated man, born into poverty Earl woods lived through the worst of American racism and segregation. He managed to put himself through college and joined the army where he became a green beret in Vietnam, in his second expedition in Vietnam he returned home with a new wife who was tiger's mother something his first wife and three kids didn't have prior knowledge of.

When tiger was born of that second marriage Earl wood was forty-three years old and was not really excited to be a father. For the early years of tiger's life being fathered meant being strapped to a high chair while his father hit golf balls in the garage. It was in watching his father play golf instead of playing as a regular kid that he developed his love for the game. For what will be the remainder of tiger's childhood his father dedicated his time to teaching him golf. he was made to spend thousands of hours watching and practicing his father's swinging technique at a military golf course close to their home, thanks to the discounted rate Earl wood enjoyed as a military man. Earl's dedication to deliberate practice is undoubtedly what made tiger wood a great golfer. Earl wood knew that golf could be mentally challenging and for his son to be so good that the golfing world couldn't ignore him he had to increase his challenges, practice needed to be tougher than the real game, and he needed to push his son to the limits and beyond.

Starting when tiger was seven Earl took extreme measures to develop his son's skills and concentration. Whenever tiger teed off earl would throw a ball at him or block his eyesight "I wanted to teach him mental toughness, if he gets distracted by the little things I did he would never be able to handle the pressure of a tournament"

As tiger got older the training became even more brutal Earl would constantly taunt his son while he practiced imagine what it will feel like for a child to hear his dad call him a "motherfucker" while he is trying to concentrate. Imagine how painful it would be to have your dad tell you to "fuckoff" or ask you "how do you feel being a little nigger" earl would go to any length even if it was unethical of a father to get a rise out of his son.

Earl often cheated when they played together supposedly to make it more difficult for Tiger to win. As Tiger reflected this was all deliberate training to become what his father wanted him to be "a cold-blooded assassin on the golf course"
Tiger narrated how him and his dad developed a code word he could use when he pushed too far in their physical or mental training. this code word was "enough" all he needed to say for his father to stop was "enough" not only did tiger never utter "enough" but two of them began to refer to it as the "e-word". The e-word to them was something only quitters say and losers believe in.
Any wonder that before he turned professional at the age of twenty in 1996, he had won all the age-grade golfing competitions he participated in.
Before turning seven he won the under-ten section of the drive, pitch and push competition held at the navy golf course. In 1984 at the age of eight he won the junior world golf championship,

a championship he went on to win six times including four consecutive wins from 1988 to 1991. Earl also confessed that tiger wood defeated him at the age of eleven with him trying his best.

On a closer examination of tiger wood's career, you would notice that even before the age of twenty when he turned professional, he might have tripled the ten thousand hours required for mastery considering the intensive deliberate training he did. That is about thirty thousand hours of intensive deliberate practice for a twenty-year-old. No wonder he "cleaned" all the age-grade championships and won the PGA tour in less than a year of going pro. Anybody who has had the privilege of watching tiger woods in live performance would have no doubt about his passion and talent but ultimately it was his brutal craftsmanship that made him what he is.

The intriguing and unconventional life of tiger wood is not exclusive to him, in the world of craftsmen this kind of lifestyle is the norm. the abnormal life that comes from dedication, hard work, receiving feedbacks and having to sacrifice pleasure is the template for all craftsmen in any field.

THE CRAFTSMANSHIP OF RONALDO

 Christiano Ronaldo was born in Madeira Portugal, his father Jose Aveiro just like Earl wood had his own demons, he was an alcoholic. He worked as a kit man for Andorinha football club and also as a part-time municipal gardener. He was born into poverty and it was in following his dad to work that he developed his almost unnatural obsession for football. He also picked up his father's work ethic in working two jobs. As a child Ronaldo played for Andorinha for three years between 1992 to 1995 before joining sporting CP who signed him after impressing on a three-day trial. The rest is history, Ronaldo has built an enviable football career for himself and is arguably the greatest footballer of all time. To attest to his craftmanship he has always attributed his success to hard work and commitment. Carlos Tevez a former teammate at Manchester united revealed in an interview "what I noticed about him and that surely all the women see is that he spends all day in the gym, it is an obsession that he has, if we trained at nine in the morning he was already there when you arrive at eight, if you arrived at seven-thirty he would already be there, I said how can you beat this guy? One day I arrived at six in the morning to do it and he was already there half asleep but he was there"

Any wonder why he has five balon d'ors, five champions leagues, won multiple league titles in different countries and is football all-time top scorer.

Ronaldo is the perfect model of a craftsman because unlike most career idols who attribute their success to mystic talent and the courage to follow their purpose in a bid to make themselves look larger than life, Ronaldo makes it obvious his craftmanship is the source of his success and passion, his work ethic is there for all to see.

In the world of sports and entertainment the use of deliberate practice is common and craftmanship to an extent is the norm but when it comes to knowledge-based workers and office workers, they don't know how to use deliberate practice to acquire career capital that would set them apart from their colleagues, this is due to very few or no avenue to express creativity or intelligence but this also presents an opportunity for those who can find rare and valuable skill in those place of work and gain mastery in them. This skill will quickly distinguish them and grant them preferential treatment (control and respect) and a deep sense of confidence in their abilities (competence). With this trait, they are bound to be passionate. It is important to note that craftsmanship can be applied to almost any field of work.

THE BOY WHO ALWAYS CAME FIRST.

During my secondary school days, I had a classmate named George who came first position in the class from my first year (JSS1) until my final year (SS3). the rest of us were left to scramble from second position backward. In my fascination with his intellectual capabilities what I came to realize was that his father was a secondary school teacher while his mum was late. As is customary of secondary school teachers, they were always very strict and have a no-nonsense approach when it came to parenting their children. George's father denied him a normal holiday. For George holidays were not much different from a school term. Holiday meant being indoors studying next term's academic work and without the pampering of his mum, he dared not to do anything else. When school resumed, he had already finished the academic work for the term, class lessons were nothing more than revision and a chance to further enforce his intellectual superiority. To make things worse while some of us slept through classes we considered boring he was awake and fully involved, asking questions and even correcting the teacher's errors, sometimes lessons felt like a one-on-one chitchat between him and the teacher. For George feedback came in the form of fatherly love he received when his dad sees his report card and the pride on his dad's face when he cleans up almost all the prizes in our class category during the annual speech and prize giving ceremony organized by the school at the end of the academic year.

If you have been paying attention to the stories on Tiger woods, Ronaldo and George you would notice a trend of an overbearing parent and discomfort. The truth is deliberate practice is very difficult and sometimes inhuman which is why they are very few craftsmen which further intensifies their distinctiveness. It is very unnatural for someone to put themselves through difficulty so as to get a rise out of themself.
Just like the mythical hydra that regenerates an extra head when its head is cut off, we human beings have redundant potentials inside of us waiting for harm to be done to us so that it can surface, so that the more we are exposed to stress the more our potentials grow. The more our skills become refined and since we are incapable of harming ourselves, we often need people or life circumstances to help us do the job. This could be an overbearing parent or trainer, being born into poverty, having a clear goal and objective, having a near-death experience, the list is endless

CONTROL: THE DREAM JOB ELIXIR

The most important trait of a great work is *control,* it is most responsible for the psychological reward of having passion for work. The author *Cal Newport* termed it the *dream job elixir.* The ability to do what you want, when you want and how you want, is the basic necessity for passion in any field of work. It is that kind of freedom that makes work not to feel like work. The quest for control in our modern world is at an all-time high and this desire has become a marketing tool among online entrepreneurs who use this desire for control to bait people into buying their course or paying to acquire a skill with the promise that once they acquire those skills, they will get paid huge amount of money while working from the beach or from the comfort of their couch.

The world is now booming with *courage preachers* who preach to young people to avoid work and follow their passion despite many passions lacking applicability to career. In a social media age where people are constantly being bombarded with the glitz and glamour of those who have compelling careers, the quest for control has never been more intensive, this has had many people fall into the *control trap*.

THE CONTROL TRAP

People fall into the control trap when they chase autonomy without having rare and valuable skills (career capital) to trade for it, this results in their quest for control subsequently becoming their undoing.

Let us take a look at the story of jane from Calvin Newport's book *be so good they can't ignore you*. Jane was a talented and intelligent student who was among the top scorers on her standardized tests and attended a competitive university. But she never loved the idea of following the traditional path of graduating from college and getting a steady paying 9-5 job, she envisioned a more adventurous life. she was an amateur cyclist who once rode a bike across the US for charity and competed in an ironman triathlon. She had a dream of circumnavigating the world's oceans and traveling without motor power across every continent, she also had other eccentric dreams like surviving the wilderness without any survival equipment for a month.

Jane didn't see the importance of her university education in her life as it played no role in accomplishing her dreams instead, she saw it as a hindrance and took the extreme decision of dropping out of school to go chase her dream a decision she would later regret. To then finance her adventurous dream, she launched her own personal blog with the hope of making at least three thousand dollars a month which she calculated would be enough to handle her basic expenses. Not only did her blog fail she confessed to having lost motivation in blogging before a substantial result could come. Her blog which she hoped will be the foundation of her empire of recurrent revenue generation featured only three posts in nine months. Jane came to the realization of the hard truth to have control over one's working life and subsequently build a compelling career that oozes passion requires more than just being courageous

Now let's compare Linda ikeji and jane with respect to their approach to blogging (control). Linda blogged for half a decade amid being involved in other endeavours that kept her afloat, she only ventured into full-time blogging when it started generating revenues, by the time she entered into full-time blogging she had accumulated years of career capital in blogging and show-business to know what works and what doesn't work.

Most importantly she started full time blogging with results and not hope or expectation as jane. Jane on the other hand ventured into full-time blogging with no career capital, her three-blog post in nine months attested to this fact. Jane only dared to jump into blogging with the hope and expectation that it will grant her control to chase an adventurous career. In the end she lost her motivation because she was not competent enough, she lacked the career capital needed in exchange for a compelling blogging career that would sponsor an adventurous life and without a university education she shot herself on the leg, the odds of making her dream life a reality has now exponentially increased.

The truth is control is very seductive, to live life on one own terms in this already constricted and templated world is a dream that will keep anybody awake at night but one needs to be very careful else become a victim of control.

AVOIDING THE CONTROL TRAP.
OBEYING THE LAW OF FINANCIAL VIABILITY

Obeying the law of financial viability is the only way to avoid the control trap it states that one should venture fully into an endeavour only when people are ready to pay for it. It encourages that in the quest for control we should try to earn it rather than trying to grasp it. When we try to earn control we tend to transition, it is in this transitioning process that we gain career capital. We learn the tricks of the trade; we practice and we examine what works and what doesn't. It is okay to want control over your work life; it is okay if you want to quit your job but instead of trying to *jump* into a more compelling career part why not *transition*. Create a transition plan it could be a decade transition plan, a five-year transition plan, a nine-month transition plan, or even a month transition plan. Any amount of time that will be enough for you to gain enough career capital in that career path and only venture into it fully when it starts yielding substantial revenue.

CONTROVERSY

Don't follow passion doesn't literally translate to consciously choosing a career path that doesn't align with your passion. What it encourages is that we should approach work whether it is in alliance with our passion or not with a deep sense of responsibility and patience instead of high expectations to find immediate purpose or enjoyment. Purpose in life is not rigid nor is it tied to a singular endeavour. You can develop purpose In in any endeavour in life as long as you stay dedicated and stay long enough to see the impact of your work on the world and in your life. It is ok to want to match work with pre-existing passion, if you manage to do that, remember there is still a lot of work to be done. If your work doesn't match your pre-existing passion there is no need to panic or become pathetic always remember it is hard to find purpose when you are at the bottom of the work food chain, be dedicated, distinguish yourself by gaining career capital, work your way up the food chain and your purpose will come finding you

LESSONS

1. Take responsibility for your passion, develop rare and valuable skills (career capital) that can be traded for a compelling career

2. Be okay with work being work, even if you are fortunate enough to make a career out of a hobby you still won't escape work

3. See passion or a deep sense of purpose as a psychological reward for being at the cutting edge of your craft (mastery) and be okay if neither is present at the beginning of your career journey

4. Be okay with criticism and failure they are vital feedbacks

5. Deliberately make your practice difficult, seek stress and discomfort in training and you will unlock new levels of your ability.

6. You are as passionate as you are competent so seek mastery

7. Don't be satisfied with being part of the system, be the system.

8. Working right trumps finding the work

9. In whatever endeavour you find yourself try
be so good that you cannot be ignored.

10.   When you want to live a job in pursuit
of a compelling endeavour do not be naïve to
think that all you need is courage instead
build an artillery of career capital while
following a transition plan.

CHAPTER FOUR

ENGAGE IN CONFLICT

He who runs away from a fight lives to fight another day

African Proverb.

DIRECT VS INDIRECT CONFLICT

As you learned in *chapter two* of this book although Jesus preached peace, he didn't scratch conflict off the menu. He sparingly engaged in any form of *direct conflict* which involved violence and the only episode of that was with the money lenders who turn a place of worship (his father's house) into a market place however he engaged in many forms of *indirect conflict* as he rebelled against the Sadducees, pharisees and taught contrarily to Jewish customs. His actions led to the success of gospel even in the face of great opposition and gave his disciples the courage to carry on when he was no longer with them, it could only be divine wisdom.

this chapter is not about encouraging you to mindlessly involve yourself in violence (direct conflict) at the slightest of provocations, there is no gain in having a bunch of enemies but the objective here is to teach you to have the courage to engage in *indirect conflict* which you can't escape in life if you want to be relevant or formidable and how to get the best out of it. They are two types of conflict which are:

Direct conflict: it involves the use of violence either physically or verbally, it is time and energy consuming. It is very chaotic and dangerous. It can have an after effect that could last a lifetime. It is a type of conflict that causes enmity between individuals and a group of people. Those who engage in direct conflict are often termed troublesome and are at risk of making a bunch of enemies but most importantly it brings about settlement and long-term peace. This type of conflict just as Jesus did should be used sparingly under extreme conditions such as violation and oppression.

Indirect conflict: this is the type of conflict you cannot escape in life if you want to be somebody meaningful in society. It involves standing by your believes no matter the opposition, setting the standard on how you want to be treated, having the courage to hold a different opinion, gently saying out your grievances in the face of provocation and sometimes denying a troublemaker the satisfaction of peace to achieve long term peace. This type of conflict is mild and not chaotic. It most often breeds understanding and respect between individuals and if done appropriately can help in averting direct conflict.

If you want to be relevant and formidable in life it is inevitable that your ego will clash with another person's ego. Some people will not like your ideas or personality due to difference in perspective and so will you. Jesus engaged in a lot of indirect conflict and it was instrumental in the propagation of the gospel.

We all want peace either peace within ourselves what I term *internal peace* or peace with the outside world what I term *external peace.* peace brings stability to our life and with that comes an enjoyable human experience. To maintain any form of peace we must deal effectively with provocations and the accompanying negative emotions. As a person starts their journey of self-development their emotional awareness increases and are able to deal more effectively with provocations. Some provocations will pass through them without causing any resentment while some won't, they will have to deal with those negative emotions that arises due to provocations they couldn't overlook and this where the purposeful use of conflict comes in. conflict then serves as channel to vent out these negative emotions that might distort a person's peace and as you have learnt it must not always be violent or aggressive but can also be an act of self-love.

THE PEACE PARADOX

The more you actively search or want peace the more it eludes you. The quest for peace can make a person to adopt a passive personality, toxic self-cautiousness and a desperate need to be liked by others. You will not be unable to hold your opinions, vent your frustration or say no to other people's unending demands. To sum up the misery you would have to live a life that you do not hold-up any form of resistance. You would have to live in a state of inferiority, anything goes when it comes to you.

The truth is peace is not something you find it is something that has to emanate from deep within you. If you are peaceful on the inside, that is being at peace with yourself (internal peace) you would be at peace on the outside, that is being at peace with those around you (external peace). The peace which you emanate will be genuine and infectious to those around you. The moment you make it a habit of feeling resentment and instead of attending to it by airing out your feelings (indirect conflict) you pretend and bury your grievances as result of feared consequences of engaging in conflict, you risk distorting the most important form of peace which is *internal peace.* people will quickly sense your desperation for stability and exploit it consciously or unconsciously this will then result in chaos in the future where you will then have no option than to become violent.

The truth is being at peace with other people (external peace) is ultimately not in your control no matter how good or diplomatic you are towards them but peace with yourself is within your control. You must see conflict as a way of venting out negative emotions which are responsible for causing internal resistance and distorting your peace. You must prioritize internal peace over external peace.

We human beings are both innocent and narcissistic, that is why we love and adore children they hold up the mirror for us. Children are unapologetically themselves; they don't try to please us; they are innocently selfish. They want what they want without consideration of their parent's mood or finances. They are capable of doing anything within their powers to get anyone to do their biddings.

We adult human beings still have this instinctive narcissistic trait in us for those born into religious homes it is repressed very early in life, they are taught to be good so that they can fit better into society, for those born into liberal homes they grow with up with unrepressed narcissism. They don't really care about being termed troublesome or being labelled as bad as long as they gain from it and won't shy away from exploiting the weaknesses of others especially does who had been taught to be good and can't cope with the ruggedness conflict brings.

For a troublesome person a perfect victim for exploitation is someone who has repressed every inch of aggression in a false exchange for peace. You must understand that human beings are not stupid, nobody gets into conflict because they enjoy conflict, everybody inherently wants peace and the stability it brings. Troublesome people create conflict because it yields good dividends for them. They get to have the attention they crave or have others surrender to their will.

 Conflict mongering is not just an individual thing it is also practiced by groups of people. In ancient times larger tribes went to war with far inferior tribes conquering them and taken hold of their possessions. A resounding victory then becomes a precursor for another tribal war.

The lesson here is not to build for yourself a reputation for being troublesome by mindlessly engaging in conflict. In fact, the more troublesome you become the more people are willing to engage in conflict with you. Most people will fancy the chance of bringing you to humility. The one who finally represses your selfishness and quenches your aggression, it will be a badge of honour for them, since most people would have been tired of your excesses and will be rooting for them.

The lesson here is to be a genuinely peaceful and virtuous person who is not obsessed with being peaceful and do not by all means possible try to avoid conflict especially those that would have dire consequences in the future. If someone says something that makes you feel insulted it is always better you express your feelings in the moment rather than bottle it up and risk getting in a fatal fight when the same person makes a harmless joke at your expense in the future. To be truly peaceful you must priorities internal peace over external peace. The former is in your control and the latter is not. If you are truly peaceful and contented on the inside it would be much easier to overlook other people's excesses.

You have to create a reputation there are consequences for stepping on your toes mindlessly, that even though you choose to be peaceful you do not lack aggression or incapable of putting up a resistance. This must be done with subtlety if you do it overtly you risk being seen as a trouble maker who needs to be avoided or put in place.

Engaging in conflict doesn't always mean being involved in a fight or quarrelling. It can also be as subtle as standing firmly by your beliefs even when everybody is against it, saying no to people's unending demands, being honest about how a person's action makes you feel.

In any social setting you find yourself, you must try

to the set the tune early on how you want to be treated before it gets too late. You might achieve this by subtly hinting at your independence and self-contentment, showing how competent you are, contribute with your opinions and action do not be passive, people hardly respect passive people especially within a group they see them as liabilities. It is always better to make your presence felt, then seldomly withdraw from the group into solitude making your absence felt. if you do this subtly and well enough, it will create an aura of value, people hardly fight a person of value especially if that person is on their team except in cases of jealousy. But by seldomly withdrawing from the group you hint that you are not afraid to stand alone and not desperate to be liked by others therefore not afraid of a fight even if it affects the group this will also create an aura of danger around your personality. a mix of value and danger will keep a jealous troublesome colleague at a distance or make them diplomatic towards you.

Again, you must do this covertly if it becomes an obvious front people will take you for an antisocial prick who lacks humanity and has a huge ego.

RED, YELLOW, BLUE AND GREEN

In Thomas Erikson's book *surrounded by idiots* he talked about four personality type in the work place environment and their temperament.

Each personality type he represented with the colour red, yellow, blue and green. The reds are the hot-headed bosses who are likely to cause conflict, a perfect avatar of a red person *is Mr. crabs* (a cartoon character in SpongeBob square pant). They are easily provoked and are usually avoided. The yellows are light hearted and funny, they hardly take provocations to heart and are talkative, a perfect avatar of a yellow is *SpongeBob*. People love their company because they brighten the mood anywhere, they find themselves. They are insanely creative and within a group they are the comedians. The blues are very analytic and pessimistic, a perfect example of a blue person is *squidwerld* (a cartoon character in SpongeBob square pant). They hate disorder and if provoked they will only murmur as a means of venting their frustration. Within the group they are responsible for orderliness and accountability. Then finally the greens, they are very kind and nice. If provoked they would do anything to avoid conflict, they are known for being very peaceful. They value relationship so much that they are willing to sacrifice their happiness to please other persons within the group, they are good team members. they don't fight for the spotlight rather they avoid it. they are usually shy and not strongly opinionated therefore are hardly involved in an argument. It might seem as though the green guy is immune to conflict but he is even more susceptible to a more violent conflict. In his sacrifice to keep peace what happens is that his unattended resentment piles up in some sort of resentment tank in his subconscious mind and subsequently when this tank gets filled, he pours out his frustration with utmost aggression and emotion. This this the result in fatal conflict that outweighs it cause. He risks destroying the relationship he sacrificed all his life for.

For the red boss aggression is a means of stamping her dominance and making sure her instructions are not taking lightly. Any form of conflict lacks emotional depth and its effect wear off quickly. For the yellow comedian he is naturally unbothered, he is contented and his internal peace is almost impeccable hence his creativity. he is also not immune to conflict but he also has a short memory. Because the blue guy is analytical and pessimistic, he fears the imagined consequences of engaging in conflict. Something that will cause him more harm than good so he vents his frustration covertly through murmuring and grumbling. The green guy obviously doesn't want any trouble. He values relationships and sacrifices a lot for it. Since he doesn't vent resentment often preferring to conceal it, he risks ruining the relationship he has sacrificed so much for by causing a huge chaos due to a minor issue.

WHY GOOD PEOPLE DIE AND BAD PEOPLE LIVE.

Growing up as kid my family where neighbors with a pastor and his family, my childhood memories are filled with me and my siblings playing together with the preacher's kids. They came to our house to watch movies, and we in turn went to theirs's to do the same. Their preacher dad prohibited contemporary Nollywood movies in a bid to protect his children from waywardness. They were only allowed to watch *mount Zion* films which are films produced by the Nigerian Christian movie industry.

Mount Zion films had a usual templated storyline for almost all their movies. Which is; the preacher kid who was raised with utmost moral standard and who is also a member of the church choir finally leaves the regimented confines of her parents when she goes to the university. She then makes a wayward friend often times a hostel mate. This friend then introduces her to the wayward lifestyle of late-night partying. She gets entangled with a wayward boy who gets her pregnant and urges her to abort the pregnancy, she initially refuses insisting she couldn't do such a thing due to her strong moral Christian upbringing but she would finally succumb to his advice when he reminds her of the shame it will bring to her family. She then goes ahead to abort the pregnancy if the script writers are benevolent enough, she loses her womb and if they were not, she loses her life. The end.

If the preacher kid is a boy he gets introduced into a gang by his wayward friend, he starts doing drugs, smoking and womanizing. Then the gang goes for a robbery, the preacher kid is killed in a cross fire between the gang and the police or the police arrested only him while the rest of the gang manage to escape.

You might say it is a movie and it is scripted to portray a particular message which I also agree but it also serves as a reflection of reality too. it makes me wonder those the moral correctness of good people become a course that prevents them from getting away with their vices?

To fully understand this mystery, we need to understand what being good or bad truly means. We need to understand the barest meaning of good and bad. When we say somebody is bad it actually means that person is *selfish*. Whatever bad means to you it is born out of selfishness. The man who violently rapes a teenager is selfish he doesn't care about the future of that child only his immediate pleasure. Thieves who steal people's priced possession don't care how much suffering they are causing the owners. Murderers don't care how much pain the cause loved ones. I am not a going to be judge of good or bad but whatever bad means to you has it roots in selfishness. On other hand when we say somebody is good it means that person is *unselfish*(selfless). Whatever good means to you is born out of unselfishness. the woman who donates to charity cares about the wellbeing of less privileged people. The man that doesn't cheat, steal or kill cares about the adverse effect it will have on the lives of people. So, in summary bad is selfishness while good is unselfishness.

We humans are born with both selfish and unselfish instinct, the selfish part of us is the precursor to do bad while the unselfish part of us is the precursor to do good. Our selfish instinct which inspires our tendency to do evil can also be used for our own good, it is the only way we can do good to our self. Those born into religious home with overbearing prudent parents get their selfish instinct repressed very early in life, they are taught to be good. This creates an artificial disconnection of the conscious mind from their inborn selfish instinct. The author Tim Grover refers to this selfish instinct as the *dark side.* Those born into liberal homes or those who had to fight for their survival at very young age maybe due to poverty or lack of parental attention in cases of divorce grow up with their selfish instinct unrepressed and are very expressive and adventurous.

Society tries to tame us early in life and it is for a good reason if everybody lived without virtue and a moral ethic the world would be very chaotic. Those who are taught to be good like preacher-kids feel a sense of constriction, a lack of freedom and adventure gnawing beneath their moral correctness. Since being good is about being unselfish they have a good but fragile reputation that depends on other people's validation this is also makes their personality rigid. The prudency of a well-trained kid is almost directly proportional to the repressed rebellion gnawing underneath the surface. For somebody who is considered wayward their life is full of adventure and danger, their moral code is weak, they will do anything to survive or satisfy their vanity and because they are more selfish than unselfish, they don't really care about people's opinions which only makes their reputation antifragile and personality fluid because for them nothing is repressed, they can be bad and also seldomly act virtuous.

When a preacher kid finally leaves the regimented and constricted confines of their overbearing parent and finally get to live on their own terms their feeling of lack of adventure and intense curiosity about the world create a void that needs to be filled. This then makes them easily seduced by waywardness and they tend to attract a wayward friend who satisfies those needs.

They usually mask this attraction to waywardness as them trying to be a good influence on a wayward person and subsequently make them good. They are also deceived by their ego that they can't be influenced by their new friend. What they fail to realize is that in the game of influence repression is almost incapable of influencing expression. Their rigid conservative nature does not make them good influencers.

They also make the mistake of thinking influence is a possessive and active thing but that is not the case instead influence is subtle, suggestive and insinuative, something the conscious mind can hardly detect. Influence doesn't attack our ego instead it takes holds of our subconscious mind, if influence was active, our ego will react to it the same way an antibody will react to an antigen, it will flush it out. Our human ego can't stand being under the influence of another person's ego.

The reason why good people are unable to shun vices completely and almost inevitably become victims of their vices is due to the fact that whether good or bad we all have selfishness inside of us that wants *vanity* and adventure. It can only be tamed through self-control but it cannot be deleted. The bible refers to this instinctive selfishness as "the love of the flesh" and as long as you are a human being you will always love your flesh; you will want to pleasure and excite it even if it means putting yourself in danger. This why preachers get materialistic and get a lot of criticism. Good people ultimately suffer or die from victimization which is due to two major reasons.

- **Naivety:** having no prior knowledge on vices engaged in
- **Lukewarmness:** carrying out vices half heartedly

Naivety

Since we all have a selfish side that seeks adventure, we are all prone to engage in vices but the problem is you can't rehearse it, you are either actually engaging in it or not. You can't rehearse robbing a bank you can only plan, you are either rubbing a bank or not. You can't rehearse pre-marital sex you are either indulging or not. Since a wayward person is adventurous, they have been engaging in vices all their life and have suffered consequences and enjoyed gain. They have enough experience to know what works and what doesn't and most importantly are able to keep their conscience (unselfish side) at bay. They are ready to do anything to survive even if it means victimizing other people.

When good people engage in vices, they are usually naïve, their lack of prior knowledge causes an artificial inability to do bad. Since vices can't be rehearsed, they lack experience. They are only motivated by their repressed rebelliousness. They preacher-kid who got involved in gang might not know how to handle a gun in a shoot-out or what part of town should be avoided as a member of a particular gang. The preacher's daughter who just got into the university and who is now attending late night parties and has a wayward boyfriend that gives her the adventure she seeks might have no prior knowledge of safe sex so she is at risk of getting pregnant or getting infected with STD

Lukewarmness

Another potent reason for victimization of good people is the fact that they carryout vices half-heartedly and put themselves in danger. Since only their unselfish side was given expression, they are selfless and have a huge conscience although this conscience is not powerful enough to stop them from indulging in vices it also won't let them properly execute it. They are torn between good and bad but still not in the balance. They become lukewarm trying to serve two masters at the same time, what then happens is that the carry-out vices incompletely that it comes back later to hunt them. The conscience of a gangster preacher-kid might not let him murder a bitter rival that he let them go away with a warning only for them to regroup and take their own chances on him. the preacher's daughter who got pregnant might not have the heart to carry-out an abortion and bears the mark of immorality all her life.

HOW TO AVOID VICTIMIZATION

Firstly, if you want be good and to stay good in whatever sense being good means to you. You must accept your selfish instinct and channel it to a course that is in alliance with your values, you will need that rebelliousness to be formidable for the things which are good. Selfishness itself is not a bad trait and it is the only way we can be good to ourselves. It carries our aggression, competitiveness and fighting spirit. It is the *dark side* which according to Tim Grover we must embrace. it is only in embracing it that we can then channel it for good.

Jesus channeled his aggression for a good course when he chased the money lenders out of the temple. He also rebelled against the hypocrisy of the pharisees and Sadducees. By channeling your human rebelliousness for a good course, you are able to shun the adventure that comes from vices and waywardness.

Secondly you must be aware of your rebelliousness and your susceptibility to waywardness. Do not be fooled by your egoic moral correctness that you expose yourself to undue influences or you mingle with the wrong company in a bid to show your moral superiority. Remember influence is not active neither is it possessive. Move to the extreme end of your moral correctness and stay there.

avoid Lukewarmness at all cost. Accept your constricted upbringing wear it as a badge of honour. make friends with people who share the same value as you or even better build your own team of disciples and be their muse. Embrace your boundaries and turn it into a lifestyle. If you are a preacher kid elevate the experience, redefine what it means to be a preacher-kid only then will you create your own adventure.

 Lastly if you can't abstain from vices try to know the pros and cons at least theoretically and avoid Luke warmness while you are at it. Keep your conscience at a distance execute perfectly from start to finish. This might sound very dark and immoral but remember even the bible says "you cannot serve two masters at the same" and to do that is very dangerous. Nemesis does not forgive those who carry out vices half-heartedly it sees it as an insult. Bad people do serve two masters but not at the same time.

DEALING WITH A NARCISSIST

If your relationship with someone has been reduced to frequent conflict and peaceful resolution within short intervals of time, it is a clear indicator that you are dealing with a narcissist a self-absorbed trouble maker. The seldom conflict is a marker of frequent manipulation or failed manipulation. The immediate apology such a person render is nothing more than a routine. A narcissist does not allow for the natural restoration of peace it delays their next ploy so it is better to apologies quickly so that things quickly goes back to normal. They are not after peace but immediate stability. A quick return to how things used to be is just a way of taking away the sting out of the conflict. Without any serious effect conflict tends to be a normal and habitual routine and that is the way they want it. They practice selective kindness only to do something selfish later, they keep their character ambiguous a ploy to have you tolerant of their excesses which according to them is there *weakness*. They more you try to figure them out the more opportunity they have to manipulate you. They are the first to apologize but also the first to do something insensitive. Next time you find yourself in conflict with a narcissist give quality to the conflict by bringing up past grievances as if you didn't actually forgive them don't get emotional be the knowing behind what you are doing be clear headed. Forgive them in your mind before they tender an apology and when they do tender an apology show a vague forgiveness, a kind of forgiveness that withholds the satisfaction of stability and peace, a hint that things won't quickly go back to normal.

They have to win you over to their corner; they might try to quickly win you over by an immediate kind gesture such as gifts or try to make you laugh with a joke. They might also demand for a grand favour immediately after conflict a ploy to force you to be the bigger man and take the higher road don't aggressively reject instead act genuinely uninterested. Your ambiguity will turn the tables around, now they are the ones who have to deal with you. You jingle peace in front of them but keeping it out of reach they more they try to reach for it the more sensitive and well-behaved they become and the more peaceful your relationship will be. You have to be careful not to draw the battle line, a narcissist does not have a strong moral code and can be dangerous what you ultimately want is the natural restoration of peace not further conflict. Also be careful not to fall into bitterness and unforgiveness make sure everything is a ploy not a true state of mind.

ENGAGE IN GOSSIP

When I was quite younger, I use to follow my mum to the hair salon, the owner of the salon was a jolly crippled woman who moved around the place in her wheel chair. She is very warm hearted and has this glow on her face that portrays how much she loves her job. She is a talkative a customary feature for hair dressers who are known to be hardcore gossipers. What I noticed even with my tender mind was that the atmosphere in the salon was therapeutic for these women. A handful of the women who came to the salon didn't come to make their hair but were solely there for the gossip. She will open up to them about her daily struggles as a cripple and how she will one day want to have a family of her own, her customers including my mum will be infected with her openness and vulnerability in turn they will also open up to her about some the issues in their life. They will talk back and forth on past life experiences, matrimonial life, politics, recent happenings within the neighbourhood the list is endless. When she is done with the customer, they go away feeling refreshed, life becomes more bearable for them and they can't wait to be back at the salon again.

For some of these women who came to the salon after this meeting they will finally summon the courage to stand up to their abusive husbands, for others she infected with gratitude she is crippled and still very much happy with her life why shouldn't they? For others having someone to share their struggles with make life so much bearable. Her salon was not just a salon but an epicenter for social change.

Women have been grouping and gossiping since ancient time and have been sharing their emotional pain with each other thereby forming feminine conventions that have continued to fight for women's right and equality. Any wonder why the modern convention of our present world is a feminine convention and as the world get advanced the feminine voice waxes stronger.

We humans are helplessly tribal beings, in ancient times we lived in tribes, the tribe offers us protection and a sense of belonging. If there is an enemy attacking the tribe or a wild animal attacking a member of a tribe the tribesmen unite together to fight them. This oneness makes tribesmen to find purpose in being selfless. A tribesman can voluntarily sacrifice his life to safe his fellow tribesmen or the entire tribe. This tribal instinct is still part of our human consciousness today we are more courageous to stand up for others or for a course than for ourselves.

When a person is oppressed by another person let's say a mean boss, since he is an employee, he might not have the courage to stand up to his boss and vent his frustration because he fears the consequences and he is not ready to be unemployed. He then decided to tell his colleague about the boss unacceptable behavior, his colleague in return told him about her ugly episode with the boss, they were later joined by another colleague who narrated an even uglier episode. What happens then is seeing that he is not the only victim it makes his frustrations bearable and seeing how other colleagues had suffered he begins to build courage; their collective pain sets him on purpose. He has found a course he can happily be unemployed for when next the boss put up his insensitiveness, he is surely going stand up to him and set him right even if it means losing his job.

We are not as selfish and timid as we most time think we are. We just haven't found a purpose, a course to fight for. When you engage in gossip *intentionally* and share your emotional pain with others and they do so in return we get a feeling that we are part of community and it makes our burden much easier to bear. It is like failing a test only to discover the whole class failed the test and that you are even among the top scorers. It makes more sense to die for others or for a course than to die for one's self at least others get to be alive to enjoy the liberation but if you die for yourself you are dead. So, we are instinctively more courageous to stand against the things that might hurt our family, community and our sense of purpose than ourselves. Be careful who you gossip with, it is always better to gossip with a trusted friend or even better somebody you share the same emotional pain with. They are very few things in this world that are stronger than two people united in struggle, this is how many world revolutions began.

The lesson here is to intentionally engage in gossip to build courage, to find purpose and to gain clarity and not just for the pleasure of backbiting.

CONTROVERSY

There are times when you can't afford to engage in conflict with an oppressor may be due to the fact that a brash with that person will lead to a brash with a bunch of people. Usually, this person is a figure head of a group of people. In this case play the *victim card* do it subtly and covertly if it becomes too obvious people will assume you an adult cry baby. Show how much you are suffering to those around you, draw sympathy, appeal to the rescuer in people and in no time, you would have gathered an army of avengers that will fight for your liberation without you leading them on, they will find purpose in fighting on your behalf. This idea will come to them as if it were their own choice and they will execute for you with all willingness. Usman dan Fodio was able to conquer northern Nigeria through the jihadist war by playing a victim of the oppressive Hausa leadership which burden the people with heavy taxes, by doing this he mirrored the people's oppression especially the minority Fulani tribe and they eventually went to war for him without him leading them in battle he instead maintained a consultancy role giving himself a saintly figure that was required of a religious leader. Some battles are fought with strategy rather than going toe to toe.

LESSONS

1. Let it go or let it out, don't allow negative emotions to clog inside you
2. The more you strive for peace the more it eludes you. Be contented with who you are and reduce your neediness for other people
3. If you find yourself amongst a group of people do not be passive and let other people do the work, contribute and show your value,
4. Set the tune on how want to be treated early
5. Avoid the wrong company if you want to remain truthful to your course, anybody can get influenced with the right amount of exposure and time.
6. Embrace your boundaries turn it into a lifestyle and you would find adventure.
7. It is okay if you lack the courage to stand up to a bully, talk to someone with the same problem, use gossip to build courage.
8. Sometimes allow peace and order to naturally restore itself
9. The more often you engage in indirect conflict the less likely you are going to get involved violent conflict.
10. Avoid bitterness.

CHAPTER FIVE

DO NOTHING

mastery of the world is achieved by letting things take their natural course. You cannot master the world by changing the natural way

Lao Tzu

Those who practice moderation are already in the way of Tao

Lao Tzu

WU WEI

The word *wu wei* is a Chinese word that literally translates to "do nothing or non-doing" but wu wei in actual sense does not mean not acting but it means effortless action. Being at peace with even the most frenetic of tasks in such a way that your ego dissolves and instead of carrying out the task you become one with the task such that your actions become effortless. An actor does become his character by thinking about it, he has to let go and dispense with technique and sink into the role. The dancer becomes the dance. In the western world this phenomenon is known as the *flow state* while in sports it is referred to as being in the *zone* that deep personal space where the cognitive mind is quiet and you have no thoughts, it is just you and your instincts (your nature).

Wu wei is the basic principle of Taoism the philosophy of "not forcing" the Taoist believe the more we try to intervene in the natural course of things the more we stampede it. The farmer who plants a tree can cut the weed around it, he can water it and can also add manure to it but if he over-intervenes with the natural process of growth for instance by going to pull on the sprout in an attempt to make it grow faster, he risks killing the tree by himself. Also, a parent who over intervenes in the upbringing of their children will groom rebellious children who when adults might go against their childhood values. We grow suspicious of the salesperson who overly patronizes us with their product.

The teachings of wu wei are the teaching of the flow, letting go of willful control, and the use of strategic passivity to get the best out of life. It entails stepping out of the realm of willful cognitive mind control and trusting in our instincts which is our nature to flow better with the nature of the universe. It teaches that by trying too hard we become rigid and unable to give allowance to the natural order of life which then results in struggle and chaos.

The Taoist philosopher Lao Tzu compares life to a river flowing along a course if we let go of our willfulness and flow along with the river, we will live more efficiently but if we resist the course of the river and try to swim against the tide or try to hold on to a tree branch along its path, we will live a rigid and hindered life.

Lao Tzu in his teaching urges his followers to be more fluid in their approach to life, he urged them to be like water and be one with nature "water is the softest and most yielding substance yet nothing is better than water for overcoming the hard and rigid because nothing can compete with"

Early Chinese poets likened wu wei to the best part of being drunk, the decline in rigidity and anxiety that comes from being drunk act as a form of divine protection that even if a drunkard falls into a pit he won't get hurt or get as injured as a person who is in full consciousness. In the ancient tang dynasty painters were taught to not only recreate the physical copy of nature around them but to become one with nature and feel the spirit of nature in themselves then let their inspiration flow through the brush unto the canvass. By doing this they didn't draw only the physical attributes of nature but were also able to paint the spirit of nature which is known as the *qui*. Taoist thinkers were not only interested in the finished work of art but they were more interested in the act of painting itself. An act of creativity that does not only recreate the beauty of the physical but also the sacredness of the spiritual nature of things (qui)

In our modern world today entertainers such as musicians, actors and athletes try to use marijuana and other forms of narcotic substances such as alcohol to numb the mind in a bid to express creativity. The truth is the mind is analytical but not creative. The purest form of creativity comes from the realm of the *no mind* a place where willful cognitive control dissolves. you don't need to use drugs or get high to be effortless all you need to do is *let go* and trust in your own nature (instincts) which is also in oneness with the nature of the universe.

How do we let go? Or in a more dramatic sense how do we try not to try?
 the Taoist believed that to be truly effortless and flow with life we must let go of our cognitive willfulness and trust the flow of life (the Tao) to live effortlessly we must:
- Embrace change
- Not focus on outcomes
- Practice
- Find the balance between ying and yang

Embrace change
The Taoist philosopher Lao Tzu in his writings in the *Tao Ti Ching* teaches that we should avoid

rigidity and having a stern grip on things in life. We should enjoy the impermanence of things a phenomenon known as *wabi sabi* which translates to "fleeting beauty". The Taoists believed that only things which are temporal and fleeting are truly beautiful because they represent the true beauty of nature. By not resisting change we are able to live more effortlessly. You can't hold on to your youthful years and you will certainly grow old, your beauty will fade away, and your loved ones won't live forever neither will you. This moment is fleeting and you won't get it back, by not trying to resist change we tend to enjoy what we have while it last, we are able to be mindful and enjoy the present moment the only place the flow state exists. People that are rigid and stern usually have difficulties dealing with change as they desire permanence instead of enjoying the beauty of impermanence which breeds gratitude and wholly living unfortunately for this people change is inevitable.

The living are soft and yielding, the dead are rigid and stiff. Living plants are flexible and tender, the dead are brittle and dry

Lao Tzu

Not focusing on outcomes
Obsession over future outcomes interferes with the quality of action we take in the present moment (the process).

When we desire an outcome, obsession arises and makes our cognitive mind intervene in the action we take, we then try to employ maximum effort in a way that disregards our instinct. Since the conscious cognitive mind can't be in a state of flow, we can't be effortless. Zhang zhi the Taoist philosopher admonished that the more we value the externals the worst we perform in the present moment. In the first chapter we learnt of Lao tzu's account of an archer who loses his ability to shoot when he focused too much on the prize to be won "he who is contending for a piece of earthenware puts forth all his skill if the prize be a buckle of brass he shoots timorously. if it be for an article of gold he shoots as if he were blind. The skill of the archer is the same in all cases but in the two later cases he is under the influence of solicitude and looks on the external prize as most important. All who attach importance to what is external show stupidity in themselves"

Accept your nature and trust it.
you will never come to a point in your life where you will not feel anxiety, fear or other unwanted emotions. if you try to resist them or fight them you are who the Taoist refers to as "flowing against the course of the river". Your act of resistance only energizes those emotions and causes more

instability but by accepting them as part of your human nature and not willfully trying to resist them you will be calm and undisturbed by them, and you will be able to flow in your performance even under extreme pressure especially when the stakes are high. The lesson here is to trust your instincts and let go of the need to control your nature. See the unpleasantness of your emotions as part of the way, the human way.

You should also try to accept the world as it is and see its beauty despite the suchness of reality so that instead of using force to control and solve the problems of this world you use intelligence and gentleness. Isn't it that so many times problems seem to solve themselves and by taking action we make things worse?

Find the balance between ying and yang

the Taoist believed that life is controlled by two opposing forces the *ying* and *yang*. The yang is known as the masculine force the active force of life, it is responsible for *doing* it entails things like aggression, conquering, competition, chasing ambitions, excitement, etc. while the ying is the feminine force, the receptive channel of life, it is responsible for *non-doing*.

it entails things like sobriety, calmness, meditation, listening, understanding, and gentleness. In our modern world today the yang aspect of our life is encouraged while the ying aspect of our life is discouraged but these two forces need each other to be effective. The ying (receptive life force) gives guidance to yang (active life force) which then results in us taking guided and effective action. The ying act as a connector of the physical to supernatural wisdom. The ying provides spiritual guidance while the yang is responsible for physical action. A perfect blend of the two will help us flow through the rigorousness of life. we are then not just applying force but taking guided actions which sometimes involves not taking action at all. This is one of the basic principles of Asian martial art where calmness and agility are prioritized over brute force.

Practice

to be truly effortless by practicing sounds almost impossible because practice has a lot to do with intentionality and you can't be intentional without cognitive mind interference but it is still possible, the key is to get lost in your practice without desiring to get lost in it. You can achieve this through *deliberate practice*. The easiest way to get lost in an activity is to make it a bit difficult but not too difficult, just a stretch outside of your comfort zone. If you involve yourself in a task below your skillset it will be too easy and your mind will get bored and begin to interfere, the task seems to become longer because your mind begins to take notice of time.

For example, if you go to the gym and carry a weight that is far below your strength you won't be lost in the process of weight lifting and won't flow. On the other hand, if you engage in a task that is far above your skillset it becomes too difficult and you lose motivation. For example, if a law student picks up an advanced biochemistry textbook and was intentional about reading a chapter a day, she will definitely not flow in her reading because the terms in the book will be too difficult to understand. The key to practicing effortlessness is to set up practice in such a way that it is just outside the stretch of your comfort zone and it also aligns with your skill set. A bodybuilder who can lift 50kg of weight can always decide to add an extra 2kg of weight per subsequent practice so that whenever he is in the gym, he is totally concentrated on overcoming a new challenge, he is fully present, there is a challenge to be conquered that is actually conquerable, his mind doesn't wonder. He lifts the weight in a state of flow.

DON'T THINK

Christiano Ronaldo speaking to the press after re-debuting against Newcastle united for a second spell at Manchester united confessed to being anxious before kickoff "it is unbelievable when I started the game, I was so nervous, it is normally because I did not expect that they would sing my name all through the game, I was very nervous but maybe I didn't show it but I was. The reception is incredible but I am here to win games and help the team" it is almost unimaginable to think that a thirty-seven-year-old Ronaldo who has been a professional footballer for about two decades and has scored over seven hundred career goals, won five balon d'ors and is arguably the greatest footballer of all time will develop anxiety about playing a relegation prone team like Newcastle united in the first league match of the season, the most inconsequential game of the season. Ronaldo scored two goals and won the man of the match award in that game. How was Ronaldo able to put up a stellar performance despite the enormous pressure he felt? The answer is simple "acceptance". Although Ronaldo was anxious as any of us had been in certain moments in our life but he also knew that it was part of being human, his anxiety only shows that he took his job seriously but most importantly he didn't try to interfere with his unwanted emotion. The first time he debuted for Manchester united at the tender age of eighteen he must have felt an even more powerful anxiety, same for when he debuted for Real Madrid, and also Juventus. A game against a low-level opposition like Newcastle was not going to be any different.

For most people when they begin to feel the pressure especially when the stakes become overwhelmingly high, they try to think themselves out of their emotions this then leads to mental resistance that further energizes those unwanted emotions which then paralyzes their performance. Just like the Taoist believed mastery comes from letting things take their natural course. The mastery of our mental domain as paradoxical as it might seem requires us to step back from the rigidity of the word mastery. The moment you accept your fears, anxieties and other unwanted emotions that arise especially when you are about to take a consequential action and see them as part of the human way the clearer your focus will be and the more effortless your action. When you stop to think yourself into calmness and confidence this intervention will cause them to elude you and your cognitive analytical mind that lacks creativity will take over. You will notice yourself trying too hard a phenomenon I termed *control and struggle.* When the cognitive mind is in control creativity becomes a struggle. Potentials and inspirations require spontaneity and instinctiveness to gain full expression the purest form of creativity is born out of purposelessness this is the reason why creators since ancient times were known to use narcotics to enhance their performance.

In Tim Grover's book *relentless* he narrated an account of one of his basketball clients who had an injury scare during an NBA playoff game and with another game in less than seventy-two hours he lost confidence in himself. Could this minor knock hamper his performances? The voice of the media had entered his head and he doubted his ability to lead his team to victory. He abandoned his team in the hotel and flew two thousand miles to seek guidance from his trainer. When Tim saw how much trouble his client had gone through to see him, he instinctively knew his client's problems were more psychological than physical and he cured him of all his troubles with one powerful phrase "don't think"
The truth is that we have all that we need in our nature(instincts) to achieve whatever we set our mind to do but most times it is so satisfying to hear other people's views on our abilities that it becomes the basis for how we perceive our abilities. It is good to listen to feedback but if you are ever going to achieve any form of greatness you must truly believe that nature has armed you with instincts that makes you ruthless in the face of opportunity.

You must learn to build trust in your abilities through deliberate practice in training and when it is show time you must learn to let go.

Another problem we human have is that we are afraid of our own greatness. Greatness is scary, it will cause great fear and anxiety and because we are too afraid, we stick to our comfort zone and dream very small the kind of dream that doesn't require us to be in the spotlight. We most times mask this phobia with perfectionism. We so much crave perfection that we are paralyzed to take action.

In some of Tim Grover's training sessions, he tries to remind his clients of their childhood by playing their favourite songs from when they were kids. Something that reminded them about the time when they played the game of basketball just for the fun of it, a time where they were not trying to become professionals or win a game, he takes them back to the days where it was pure instinct, when they were not *trying to do* but they were just doing.

PRACTICE PROCRASTINATION

The neurophysiology of procrastination

The prefrontal cortex (PFC) of the brain is responsible for the executive functions of the brain such as planning, decision making, organization, problem-solving and carrying out highly skilled movement. The prefrontal cortex is responsible for rationality. Then there is the limbic system which is one the oldest part of the human brain (paleo cortex) it is located at the base of the cerebral cortex just above the brainstem (midbrain, medulla oblongata, cerebellum and the beginning of the spinal cord) it forms the core of the brain. The limbic system is responsible for all emotions such as pleasure, desire and a feeling of reward, it is also responsible for behavior, memory and also acts as a relay center for impulses (due to the presence of the thalamus). The limbic system is much more developed compared to the prefrontal cortex and also impulses first relay at the limbic system before going to the prefrontal cortex. Since impulses first relay at the limbic system, it is easier to react to the reward of an immediate impulse than to delay gratification and make a rational decision. So, we tend to attend to tasks that give immediate rewards however irrelevant it might be than to attend to tasks that will give gratification in the future. We might tend to procrastinate a school assignment that its reward comes at the end of the semester and be more interested in watching a Netflix movie which will immediately cause a release of dopamine into our system giving us an instant feeling of gratification. Sometimes the PFC manages to win this battle and we take a more rational decision but it's most times difficult and requires a lot of discipline. What this teaches us is that our mind is rigged to procrastinate, it is a primal part of our nature to avoid rigorous work and seek pleasure. To be able to flow with our nature and accomplish tasks more effortlessly we have to find a way to use procrastination to our advantage. To live productively we need to learn how to use procrastination rather than combating it and we can achieve this in two ways

- **Negotiating with the mind:** the Pomodoro technique

- **Tricking the mind:** structured procrastination

The Pomodoro technique

The Pomodoro technique was invented by Francesco Cirilo in the early 1990's he named the technique after the tomato-shaped timer he used as a university student. This technique is useful in carrying out large and tedious tasks, the theory behind the Pomodoro technique entails dividing a task into intervals of twenty-five minutes of work (Pomodoro) and five minutes of rest. To get the best results you must work with optimum concentration during the work period and reward yourself with rest once the work interval is over, this could be taking a walk from a place of work to reward yourself with a treat. The advantage of the Pomodoro technique is that it allows a person to maintain a good amount of concentration over a long period and all that is needed to practice this technique is just a timer. You can tweak the time intervals to suit your attention span or how you want to approach the task. It could be an interval of one hour of work to twenty minutes of rest depending on what suit you.

The Pomodoro technique is a brilliant way of negotiating with our minds because we get to give ourselves an immediate reward of rest for our work. Which makes our mind cope better with the rigorousness of the task. In some sense, we are still procrastinating just that we are now procrastinating in between work intervals. A literal combination of ying and yang.

Structured procrastination
Another way of making the most out of procrastination is by tricking our brain into using one task to procrastinate the other. If you list a number of tasks according to the order of priority you are most likely to be motivated to do the less rigorous ones at the bottom. So, let us say you start doing the first task because it is most important or urgent then after a period of time due to its rigorousness you find yourself dreading the task you can then switch to another task say the one at the bottom of your priority list which is easier and gives immediate gratification. What you are then doing is using a task to procrastinate another. this will exponentially increase your productivity. By the time you manage to finish your first task, you might have also finished five other tasks.

Almost every ten pages of this book were written between me going for a walk, playing football, scrolling through social media and taking a nap. Most of the compelling ideas in this book came from the walks I took or a quote I saw on Twitter that sparked an idea. I could have written this book in a month but I knew if I did that it will not convey all my ideas. I needed time to write and I also needed time to chill and do regular stuff although I did all these with a deadline in mind. the author Austin kleon confessed in his book *steal like an artist* to get his best ideas when he got bored which is why he never takes his shirt to the dry cleaners in his words "I love ironing my shirt it is so boring, I almost always get good ideas"

Effective productivity comes from the balance of doing and non-doing (ying and yang) the ideas that motivate the actions we take comes mostly when we are at rest and also the energy, we need to execute a task. If we rush through a task and get it done as quickly as possible, we are at risk of not doing it to the best of our abilities, and major ideas might escape our thinking. Procrastination can also act as feedback; we procrastinate most times because we lack ideas

SURRENDER TO A HIGHER POWER

I can still remember vividly seeing my mum carry my baby sister on her back and crying to the motor pack to pick up a bus to Makurdi. She just received a call that my dad had been admitted to the hospital. A few days later she came back wailing accompanied by a crowd of mourners, my dad had just passed away in the nick of his prime leaving behind a very young family of four kids and a young wife. My dad was the best father any child could wish for. He lost both of his parents as an infant and was raised by his three elder sisters, so he made it his life purpose to be the best father he could possibly be to his children. Never came back from work without bearing gifts, promised me and my siblings the best things in life, kept us daydreaming about our future and then he passed on. It was a very bleak period for my family, so many questions left unanswered, and so many promises left unfulfilled.

What kept us strong was the belief that an unfailing hand rested on the wheels and that in the grand scheme of the all-knowing supernatural being it would be for good. This faith preserved our sanity. It was our belief in God that kept us calm and resilient through the storm. Even though we found it hard to come to acceptance with our demise we believed that there was some deeper purpose behind our suffering.

My mum was always listening to *God will make a way* a song by Don Moen, it was her ringtone but it quickly became a family mantra.

Since ancient times man had always believed in a higher power, a wise being that was in control of what was not in their control. It was the only way the world could be sane. It is no surprise they overcame the horrors of plagues, wars and holocausts with so much poise and diligence. To deal with the immense complexity, difficulty and potential emptiness of life with nothing but our own mind can lead to nihilism and a deep sense of victimization. It is the belief that even though our immediate observational experience may be unacceptable it is for the greater good that keeps us antifragile and calm. Without surrendering we risk developing a huge ego that becomes our master, we will be a slave to our urges and place value in mundane things. There will be no power to restrain our vanities. We will force our way through life and ruin the natural other of things. we won't be able to maintain calmness in face of adversity or under overwhelming pressure because we had put the results of outcomes in our own hands. Only those who truly surrender to God are conversant with the flow state. You need divinity to override the tyranny of your cognitive mind and bring it to peace. The stoics believed in God not because they had evidence that God exists but because they knew that to fully focus on what you can control which is the core teaching of their philosophy one must surrender to a higher power the things that are outside of their control.

The world is too ambiguous to try to figure it out alone with the mind. There is tranquility in believing in something higher than ourselves. That richness is always open to you, all you have to do is let go and believe that God knows why and he is the ruling logic behind the workings of the universe, just surrender.

CONTROVERSY

The concept of *doing nothing* is not in any way an encouragement to live a passive and minimalist life. The lesson here is to use wise strategic passivity instead of brute force to maneuver through life, by doing that you save yourself time and energy. It is an invitation to trust in your instinct and your divine nature which is the only way to avoid the tyranny of your cognitive analytical mind. *Doing nothing* does not mean not working hard but it means coating your efforts with "surrenderedness" so that you can maintain calm and poise even under overwhelming pressure and adversity.

LESSONS

1. To attain mental mastery, you must become an unfocused observer of your emotions. It requires you not to be a master but an observer

2. *Not doing* is equally as important as *doing* Learn to carry out the most consequential action with a sense of purposelessness. Focusing too much on outcomes most times reduces the quality of the outcome

3. The best way to avoid procrastination is to practice it, let it be part of the schedule

4. Greatness is scary, the spotlight will bring great anxiety and you should be okay with that

5. Do not willfully try to get rid of your unwanted emotions it will only energize them.

6. To truly be calm in the face of adversity and pressure you must surrender the outcome to the divine

7. If you want to flow at a task or practice, make it a little difficult

8. The flow state only exists in the present moment, when the mind is totally focused on the task at hand

9. No matter the suchness of your present reality, always remember an unfailing hand rests on the wheel. let this bring you solace

CONCLUSION

Dear reader, our counterintuitive wisdom-journey in this book has come to an end. We have seen what made the greats become achievers and also how the resilient were able to last long in their resolutions and as we have realized it is not conventional knowledge. As the proverb says "you can force a horse to the stream but you can not force it to drink water" and so the knowledge in this book is up to you to apply in your daily life and live up to your full potential. We live in a chaotic yet beautiful world, sometimes this chaos is external but most times this chaos happens inside of our mind especially when fate begins to test us, the challenges of life are there for our capacitation, it is all part of the journey and how you deal with these challenges determine your growth. Life is a game that plays us but with mastery comes the ability to play the game of life and be a ruthless winner. I encourage you to read again and again until the lessons in this book becomes innate in you.

ACKNOWLEDGEMENT

I want to first of all show gratitude to God almighty for giving me the grace and wisdom to write this book, I couldn't have done it without divine help. I want to thank everybody who helped me in making this book a possibility, my *antifragilista* brother Nathaniel first and foremost for his support and encouragement to me following my own path without fear. My gratitude also goes to my mum, who has always shown me unconditional love. Her love and uprightness have been quintessential and also the basic raw material for this book. I am also grateful to my two wonderful sisters Chelsea and favour who have been great listeners, they were the perfect outlets for my ideas. To my extended family who in one way or another other has been a source of support, I say thank you. I want to say a big thank you to my readers at my Facebook blog *Zenfootball* they gave me a chance to workshop many of the ideas in this book. My final gratitude goes out to the thinkers, philosophers, athletes, authors and businessmen, and businesswomen whose ideas and life principles make up this book. It would never have been possible without them but most importantly their insights and ideas have made my life better. I am grateful to the heroes and villains in the stories written here, their successes and failures serve as a guide for anyone in pursuit of happiness, fulfillment, and clarity.

ABOUT THE AUTHOR

Anawo Mathias hails from the middle belt of Nigeria. he is a writer,a footballer, a mental health enthusiast, and has a degree in Human anatomy. He is the owner of the Facebookblog *zenfootball* which is a blog that helps in developing the minds of footballers (athletes) and regular people so that they can become the best they can be.

As a student of life, he has made it his life mission to share his lessons with the world in a bid to reduce human suffering, create clarity and raise a generation of pragmatic and resilient individuals.

Contact the author

anawomathias@gmail.com

twitter: @AnawoMathias

Instagram: @Matsben_official

Facebook: @zenfootbal

BIBLIOGRAPHY

1. **Be so good they can't ignore you**---Calvin Newport

 2. **Stillness is the key**—Ryan Holiday

3. **The obstacle is the way**—Ryan Holiday

4. **Ego is the enemy**—Ryan Holiday

5. **The power of Now**—Eckhart Tolle

6. **The subtle art of not giving a fuck**—Mark mason

7. **Relentless**----Tim Grover

8. **Good to great**--- Jim Collins

9. **Outliers** ---Malcom Gladwell

10. **The monk who sold his Ferrari**---- Robin Sharma